SUPER-SPEEDY COLLEGE COOKBOOK

SUPER-SPEEDY
COLLEGE
COOKBOOK

HEALTHY RECIPES IN 20 MINUTES OR LESS

MICHELLE ANDERSON

ROCKRIDGE
PRESS

For general information on our other products and services or to obtain technical support, please contact our Customer Care Department within the United States at (866) 744-2665, or outside the United States at (510) 253-0500.

Rockridge Press publishes its books in a variety of electronic and print formats. Some content that appears in print may not be available in electronic books, and vice versa.

TRADEMARKS: Rockridge Press and the Rockridge Press logo are trademarks or registered trademarks of Callisto Media Inc. and/or its affiliates, in the United States and other countries, and may not be used without written permission. All other trademarks are the property of their respective owners. Rockridge Press is not associated with any product or vendor mentioned in this book.

Interior and Cover Designer: Brian Lewis
Art Producer: Tom Hood
Editor: Van Van Cleave
Production Editor: Jenna Dutton
Production Manager: Michael Kay

Illustrations © 2021, Tom Bingham, pp 6, 7, 13, 14, 15, 40. Photography © 2021 Annie Martin, cover and p. 94; Tanya Zouev/StockFood, p. vi; Michael Wissing/StockFood, p. x; Gräfe & Unzer Verlag/mona binner PHOTOGRAPHIE/StockFood, p. 18; für ZS Verlag/Coco Lang/StockFood, p. 22; Great Stock!/StockFood, p. 38; Sporrer/Skowronek/StockFood, p. 44; Hélène Dujardin, p. 58; Cameron Whitman/Stocksy, p. 62; Larissa Veronesi/StockFood, p. 76; Rua Castilho/StockFood, p. 82; Marija Vidal, p. 106; Tim Pike/StockFood, p. 124; The Picture Pantry/StockFood, p. 134.

ISBN: Print   978-1-64876-030-3
          eBook 978-1-64876-031-0

R0

FOR MAC AND COOPER.
I HOPE THIS HELPS YOU
FEED YOURSELVES WHEN
YOU'RE AWAY AT SCHOOL.

CONTENTS

NAME: ....

GRADUATION DATE: ....

MAJOR: ....

**FAVORITE
DISH TO COOK:** ....

GO .... **!**

CHAPTER ONE

THE
TIME
OF YOUR
LIFE

1

MAKING EVERY SECOND COUNT

Welcome to college! You may be reading this as a new student starting an exciting adventure or as a current student continuing your journey. No matter what stage you are in, the goal of this book is to introduce you to speedy, delicious recipes you can whip up in your dorm room or in a communal or apartment kitchen. College can be overwhelming at times, so knowing how to make quick, no-fail, nourishing recipes can take the stress off your already full plate. Plus, learning to prep and cook meals is a valuable life skill that will serve you well even after you graduate.

Don't worry if cooking is completely unfamiliar to you; the dishes in this book take only 20 minutes from start to finish and often use precooked ingredients such as ramen noodles, chicken breasts, beans, and rice. The recipes consider equipment allowed in dorm rooms or give alternative methods to make the recipe if certain appliances aren't allowed. You will learn about adding spice blends to boost flavor profiles and about creating nutritious meals in the microwave or blender.

The recipes have been tested to suit your lifestyle and palate. However, keep in mind some basic rules when cooking for yourself:

READ THROUGH THE RECIPE FIRST. This will ensure you have all the ingredients, know what needs to be done, and how long the recipe will take.

GET OUT ALL YOUR INGREDIENTS. Arrange all the ingredients needed, and prep anything that needs to be chopped or sliced. This routine will save time, and you won't get caught scrambling for ingredients or utensils in a recipe step.

SUPERVISE. Do not leave food unattended when cooking and keep cooking areas clear of combustibles.

KNOW HOW TO HANDLE A FIRE. If you have a grease fire, smother it with a pot lid or potholder; never spray a fire extinguisher at it or try to douse it with water. Turn the burner off. If you have a microwave fire, close the appliance door and unplug it. Do not use the appliance again.

PROTECT YOUR COUNTERS OR COOKING AREA. Get a heatproof surface such as a large ceramic tile to place your equipment on when in use.

BE CAREFUL WITH THE ELECTRICITY. Do not plug multiple appliances into an extension cord, or you could overload the electrical outlet. Unplug your appliances when they are not in use.

REMEMBER TO CLEAN. Wash your cooking equipment, utensils, dishes, and cutting boards in hot, soapy water immediately after using them (and they have cooled down). Wipe down all areas used for prep and cooking.

EQUIPMENT & TOOLS

There are no hard and fast rules for approved cooking equipment at colleges or universities. Each place is different, so check your orientation package and the school website to see what is allowed in your dorm. Before bringing any equipment, check the wattage limits because some microwaves have higher requirements. The range of possible accepted equipment is extensive. Consider buying appliances with an automatic shutoff for safety. If you're staying in a dorm with a communal kitchen or rent an apartment with a full kitchen, then the kitchen's your oyster! The recipes in this book span any circumstance, and many have creative tips for adapting to different equipment.

HOW TO COOK IN COLLEGE WHEN YOU HAVE . . .

. . . **Nothing at all:** While obviously not ideal, never fear; you can still make delicious meals for yourself! Many recipes in this book can be made with no cooking equipment, such as sandwiches, salads, snacks, and overnight oats. Check out the Berry-Granola Parfait (page 23), Bistro Chicken Caesar Sandwich (page 48), and Speedy Summer Gazpacho (page 74) to get started.

. . . **A microwave and a mini fridge:** This combination is common in most colleges and often can be rented directly from the school. Microwaves are very versatile, and you can make everything from breakfast to dessert and even pasta! Check out the Banana French Toast (page 30), Vegetarian Taco Bowl (page 43), and Four-Cheese Mac & Cheese (page 79) for inspiration.

WAIT! DON'T MICROWAVE THAT

ALUMINUM FOIL

CHINESE TAKEOUT CONTAINERS

DISHES WITH METALLIC TRIM

HARD-BOILED EGGS

PLASTIC CONTAINERS

STYROFOAM

TRAVEL MUGS

YOGURT CONTAINERS

AND FINALLY, NEVER RUN YOUR MICROWAVE WITH NOTHING IN IT BECAUSE DOING SO CAN WRECK THE APPLIANCE.

. . . **An electric burner:** This is like a handy portable stovetop, so the sky's the limit if you have a pot and skillet. You can cook eggs, pancakes, soups, sandwiches, and almost anything else. Serve up Bean & Veggie Chili (page 73) and Skillet Marinara (page 89) to impress your roommates.

. . . An electric kettle: Because kettles boil water, you can make ramen, soups, oatmeal, coffee (with a French press), and teas. If your kettle is the type that has a removable lid, you can also boil eggs in it. Enjoy Single-Serve Cheesy Lasagna (page 84), Instant Veggie Noodle Soup (page 69), and Mediterranean Couscous Salad (page 45) courtesy of this humble appliance.

. . . A coffeemaker: Believe it or not, you can use a coffeemaker to make more than just coffee! This appliance is basically a pot and hot plate, so with a little ingenuity, you can hard-boil eggs, cook poultry or fish, make soup, or cook pasta. Check out Cobb Lettuce Wraps for the eggs (page 56) and Homestyle Chicken Alphabet Soup (page 65) for soup.

. . . An oven: You have hit the jackpot, cooking-wise, with an oven. *Don't have a stovetop? See the dorm hacks on page 7.* You will need a skillet, pot, baking sheet, and casserole dishes to take full advantage of an oven. Satisfy your cravings with Cheesy Quesadillas (page 83) and Ketchup-Glazed Meat Loaf (page 116).

. . . A toaster or toaster oven: A toaster oven is basically a mini oven. Broiling, baking, frying, roasting . . . you can do it all, depending on the appliance. Get cooking with the Hearty Tuna English Muffin Melts (page 52), Chickpea Salad on Toast (page 51), and Mini Pita-Pocket Pizzas (page 54).

TOOLS TO GET NO MATTER WHAT . . .

You don't need anything elaborate to create the recipes in this book, but here is some essential equipment you'll want to have on hand:

BLENDER: This book has smoothies, soups, and dips that need blending. At a minimum, get one that is powerful enough to crush ice.

CUTTING BOARDS: Always sanitize the board with hot, soapy water when switching between produce, poultry, fish, or red meat, to avoid cross-contamination.

HIGH-QUALITY KITCHEN KNIVES: You won't spend hours on prep, but have at least one larger chef knife and a small paring knife.

MEASURING CUPS AND SPOONS: Accurate measurement is crucial for recipe success. Purchase a set of wet and dry measuring cups and measuring spoons.

MICROWAVABLE CONTAINERS: You will need a large mug, two 8-ounce ramekins, and a couple 1-quart baking dishes made of silicone, glass-ceramic ware, or heat-proof glassware.

NESTED STAINLESS-STEEL BOWLS: A set of three stacked bowls—a 6-cup, 4-cup, and 2-cup capacity—will handle all your recipes.

WIDE-MOUTH MASON JARS: Some recipes such as soups, overnight oats, and salads are made directly in mason jars, so get at least four 1-quart jars with wide tops.

DON'T FORGET THE SMALL STUFF . . .

In addition to your appliances and other equipment, be sure to stock up on a few kitchen basics to get you started:

ALUMINUM FOIL, PLASTIC WRAP, AND SEALABLE PLASTIC BAGS

BOX GRATER

CAN OPENER

DISH SOAP, SPONGES

DISH TOWELS

PEELER

PLATES, BOWLS, FLATWARE, BEVERAGE GLASSES (FOR SERVING)

POT HOLDERS

SPATULA

TONGS

FOOD STORAGE CONTAINERS

WHISK

WOODEN SPOONS

If you have access to a stove or full kitchen, buy a few basic pots and pans:

10-INCH NONSTICK HEATPROOF SKILLET

2-QUART SAUCEPAN

BAKING SHEET

LARGE 8-QUART POT

SMALL NONSTICK SKILLET

DORM HACKS

Depending on your school's rules, you might have to get creative when making your food. Many recipes will have dorm hacks at the end, but here are a few more to get you started:

INSTEAD OF A STOVETOP . . . Use an electric burner (hot plate), coffeemaker, electric tea kettle, or microwave.

INSTEAD OF A TOASTER OR TOASTER OVEN . . . Use an electric burner, waffle iron, clothes iron, or microwave.

INSTEAD OF AN OVEN . . . Use a toaster, toaster oven, microwave, or waffle iron.

HEALTHY, CONVENIENT INGREDIENTS

The foundation of successful cooking is the ingredients, which are especially important for quick and healthy meals. In this section, I'll go over some pantry and perishable ingredients that you will use again and again to create nutritious meals.

PANTRY

Your pantry might mean a designated shelf in your room or cabinet space in a communal kitchen. Either way, here are some products you should always keep stocked.

WHOLE GRAINS. Oats, rice, bread, and quinoa are versatile base ingredients for many recipes, and they are filling and quick to make. Try to have a loaf of whole-grain bread and microwavable, precooked rice packs along with dry, uncooked grains on your shelf.

MARINARA SAUCE: Premade tomato sauce is convenient, tasty, and ready to eat! Look for products with few ingredients, all of which you can pronounce, and no added sugar for the healthiest choice.

PASTA: Macaroni, spaghetti, penne, rotini, and, of course, ramen are all staple items in this book and college cooking in general. Try to pick up whole-grain or veggie pasta for a little boost in nutrition.

BROTH: Veggie and chicken broth are used in many dishes in the following chapters, so grab a couple boxes or cans for convenience. You can find sodium-free or reduced-sodium products for a healthier option. Premade flavored broths can be delicious, but use them sparingly because they are high in sodium.

CANNED LEGUMES: Casseroles, chili, hummus, and even desserts can have fiber- and protein-rich beans in them. Keep black beans, chickpeas, and white beans in your pantry and buy no- or low-sodium products, if possible. Drain and rinse before using them.

FRIDGE

You might not have a fridge in your room, but many colleges provide communal kitchens, so you can put a few items in the fridge and freezer (labeled with your name!). Some ingredients to keep in the fridge include:

PLAIN GREEK YOGURT: Yogurt is not only a tasty snack but it is also the ideal ingredient for smoothies, parfaits, and curries. Pick up full-fat yogurt because low- or no-fat has added ingredients and sugars you do not want to eat.

EGGS: This ingredient will find its way into breakfast, salads, main meals, and sweet treats. You can even hard-boil some eggs for a grab-and-go high-protein snack. Perfection!

MINCED GARLIC IN A JAR: Garlic adds a distinct, delectable flavor to savory recipes even in small amounts, but it can be a pain to chop or mince. A small jar of minced (not pureed) garlic is an easy alternative, and refrigerated, it lasts for up to one month after opening.

DAIRY OR NONDAIRY MILK: The variety of milk available at the store is vast, so pick up a half-gallon container for all your recipe needs or as a nutritious beverage. The unsweetened nondairy milks (plain and vanilla) are the best choices if you want to control your sugar intake.

CHEESE: Many recipes use mouthwatering cheese, including pasta, sandwiches, and breakfast, so pick up a block and shred and slice as needed. Unless cream cheese, goat cheese, or Parmesan is called for, any cheese can be substituted in this book's dishes.

FROZEN FRUIT AND VEGGIES: The quality of frozen produce is just as good as fresh. Fruit is tasty in smoothies, crisps, and baked oatmeal, and vegetables complete the flavor of soups, pasta, stews, and casseroles.

SPICE BLENDS ARE YOUR FRIEND

What is an inexpensive way to add heaps of flavor to your meals? Spices and herbs! Many of the recipes in this book utilize different individual products to boost a dish's taste, but blends are even more convenient. Some commonly used spice blends include Italian, everything bagel, Tex-Mex, herbes de Provence, jerk spice, and garam masala, which are all available in most grocery stores. You can make them yourself before you come to school—there are countless recipes online—but store-bought is just as good. You can substitute a spice blend in most of the recipes in this book, such as Italian for basil or oregano, garam masala for cumin or coriander, and instead of thyme or rosemary, use herbes de Provence.

SMART SHOPPING

Shopping for yourself might be a new activity, but with a little planning it can be simple and affordable. Here are some smart shopping tips to get you started:

PLAN AHEAD: Planning is key to efficient and cost-effective shopping. Planning means deciding what meals you'll make during the week, creating a shopping list, and checking your fridge or pantry for items you already have on hand. A list will also help curb impulse buying. Organize your list into categories such as "produce" and "frozen" and "pantry." Try not to shop when you are hungry or tired.

BUY PRODUCE IN SEASON: Fruit and veggies are less expensive and taste best in season. Look for deals in your local supermarket and at farmers' markets if you have one nearby. Pick up fresh fruit for nutritious snacks, but to avoid spoilage, don't stock up on items you don't need.

SHOP IN BULK: Buying in bulk is a good strategy for items you frequently use like the ones in the Pantry section (page 8), but not for everything. If you share food, bulk purchasing is economical. Your money will go a long way with bulk pasta, frozen veggies or fruit, marinara sauce, and rice.

KNOW HOW TO SHOP FOR ITEMS: Pick from the back of the produce bins, shelves, and coolers to get the freshest products. Read the expiration dates as well, and shop the perimeter of the store for healthier options.

SET A BUDGET AND STICK TO IT: It can be easy to spend too much money on food, especially for new cooks and shoppers. Make a budget and stick with it. As you shop, use your phone or your head to keep track of what you're spending. Look for generic brands, which are often the same as name brands but cheaper.

MAKING FOOD LAST LONGER

Food has a lot of different labels that can be confusing and make us think we've wasted food when it's actually still good. First, if a food has a "best-before" date, you can still eat it after the date if the food looks and smells fine. However, the "use-by" date on fresh food such as meats, poultry, dairy, eggs, and fish *is* something to pay attention to because these dates are safety-related. If you do not eat the food by the use-by date, throw it out. Below are tips to save even more time, money, and food.

COOK OR FREEZE FOODS: If you have ingredients reaching their end date, cook or freeze them. Cook chicken breasts or ground beef, cool, label, and store them in the freezer in sealed bags for up to three months.

WASH YOUR PRODUCE AS NEEDED: Wash your fruits and veggies right before using them, or they will spoil more quickly.

DIP BERRIES IN A MILD VINEGAR SOLUTION: This is the one exception to the washing rule: Berries can go bad quickly, so wash them in a 1:3 vinegar to water solution. Dry them thoroughly on paper towels and pack them in a container in the fridge.

KEEP GRAINS IN AIRTIGHT JARS OR CONTAINERS: Grains can spoil if they are in contact with any moisture, so transfer them to containers with lids or sealable plastic freezer bags.

STORE LETTUCE IN A KITCHEN TOWEL: Spread out a kitchen towel or paper towels and scatter the lettuce leaves over it. Roll the towel up, creating a bundle, and store it in the refrigerator. Change the towel every few days.

STORE YOUR PRODUCE CORRECTLY: Some fruits and veggies, such as bananas and onions, produce ethylene gas. This gas accelerates spoilage, so store this produce away from other foods. Keep bananas as a bunch and wrap the stalks tightly in plastic wrap (rewrap when you remove a banana). Items like onions, tomatoes, potatoes, apples, avocados, bananas, and lemons can all be stored outside the fridge in a cool spot or at room temperature.

TIME-SAVING KNIFE SKILLS

To ensure you don't spend hours in the kitchen prepping, you will need to know how to prepare at least a few items efficiently. Knowing what to do with common ingredients such as onions, tomatoes, and scallions can save you time and eliminate some frustration.

HOW TO DICE AN ONION

This technique will work with any type of onion, so study up!

1 Cut off the top of the onion where the stem is located.

2 If you are only using half the onion, leave the skin on while you slice it in half vertically through the root. Then peel the half you are using and leave the skin on the unused half. Place the unused half in a sandwich bag, seal, and place in the refrigerator. If you are using

the whole onion, peel off the whole onion's papery skin, and then cut the peeled onion in half vertically through the root.

3 Place half the onion on the cutting board so that the cut, flat side touches the board. Holding the root end firmly at the top of your board, cut the onion vertically

CONTINUED ▶

toward the root in ¼-inch slices, leaving the root intact. The onion should look like a fan.

4 Rotate the onion half by 90 degrees, hold it by the intact root, and slice across the vertical cuts in ¼-inch slices to create an even dice until you reach the root.

5 Repeat with the remaining onion half, if using.

HOW TO CUT A TOMATO

The best knife for slicing tomatoes is a serrated knife because tomato skin can be surprisingly tough. Regardless of the way in which you want to slice the tomato, start by placing the tomato stem-side up and use a paring knife or the end of a peeler to remove the fruit's flat stem. This process is called hulling.

TO SLICE THE TOMATO: Turn the tomato on its side and slice through it, starting from the stem side and moving toward the bottom, to create slices, thick or thin, depending on your needs.

TO DICE THE TOMATO: Slice the tomato as above, then cut the slices into strips and then cut them again crosswise to create an even dice.

TO QUARTER THE TOMATO: Cut the tomato in half from top to bottom and then cut each half to make quarters. You can cut each quarter in half to create eighths.

HOW TO SLICE A SCALLION

This technique is used to prepare scallions two ways—chopped and thinly sliced—for the scallions used in the recipes in this book. The difference is just the width of the slices.

1   Wash the scallions and remove any limp green parts.

2   Place however many scallions you need on a cutting board and cut off the top 2 inches or so of the green parts and discard.

3   Cut the root section off the white part right above where it ends, about ¼ inch.

4   Lay the scallion(s) horizontally on the cutting board with the white end on the side you hold your knife.

Hold the scallion(s) in place with your nondominant hand, taking care not to crush them, and cut the scallion by sliding the knife toward you, creating slices. Slices about ¼ inch are "chopped" and ⅛ inch or thinner are "sliced."

5   Continue down the scallion, moving the hand holding the vegetable down as well. If you only need the greens, stop where the scallion turns white.

ABOUT THE RECIPES

Now we get into the fun part! The recipes in the next chapters are designed to be fast, simple, and delicious. They use few ingredients and take 20 minutes tops. They also come with special features to further ensure your culinary success:

MASTERING THE BASICS. Each recipe chapter starts with a staple dish, such as a Mason Jar Salad (page 40) or Buddha Bowl (page 78) with a walkthrough formula, including delicious variations.

DORM-FRIENDLY LABELS AND TIPS. Any recipe that is dorm-friendly—requiring no cooking or using a common dorm-friendly appliance such as a blender or microwave—will have a dorm-friendly label. Other recipes will feature tips to adapt them for a dorm.

EASY-PEASY HACKS. At the end of each recipe, you will see tips designed to make your cooking life easier. These tips include:

- Smart Shopping: This tip tells you which ingredients can be replaced with store-bought ones or provides a suggestion about where to get a particular ingredient.

- Dorm Hack: This tip instructs you on how to adapt the recipe from a skillet or oven to a microwave or coffeemaker. These tips might not match up with your approved dorm equipment, but they will give you a good sense of what's possible.

- Make It Yourself: Some recipe components can be made rather than store-bought. This tip outlines simple recipes for commonly used ingredients, such as pesto or salsa.

- Love Your Leftovers: These tips show you how to use up leftovers, or how to use leftovers to make a new meal.

Now that you've learned the basics, let's jump into the recipes!

BERRY-VANILLA GREEN SMOOTHIE, PAGE 21

BREAKFAST

MASTERING THE BASICS: EGGS

Learning basic egg cooking techniques will give you an excellent foundation for many delicious recipes, both in this book and your own experiments. Here are some of the best techniques to use when making nutritious, quick college meals:

SCRAMBLED: Mix 3 eggs and 2 tablespoons of milk together in a small bowl. Melt 1 tablespoon of butter in a medium skillet over medium-low heat on a stovetop or hot plate. Pour in the eggs and cook until barely set, gently scraping the eggs to the center with a spatula to create fluffy curds.

MICROWAVE SCRAMBLED: Whisk together 3 eggs and 1 tablespoon of milk and pour it into a butter-greased microwave-safe bowl. Microwave on high for 1 minute, stir, and microwave for 15-second intervals (about 30 seconds total), until cooked through and fluffy.

HARD-BOILED: Put up to 4 eggs in a medium saucepan and fill the saucepan with water until the eggs are covered by about 1 inch. Place the saucepan on medium-high heat on a stovetop or hot plate and bring it to a boil. Boil for 1 minute and remove the saucepan from the heat. Let it stand covered for 10 minutes, drain, and run the eggs under cold water to make peeling easier.

COFFEEMAKER HARD-BOILED: Put 3 to 4 eggs in the coffeemaker pot and fill the water reservoir with enough water to cover them by about 1 inch. Turn the appliance on and let the water run through. Let the eggs sit in the water for about 15 to 20 minutes, drain, and cool.

BERRY-VANILLA GREEN SMOOTHIE

Smoothies are my everyday breakfast because they are tasty, quick, and start my day with a healthy portion of veggies. Just after I pour the smoothie into my glass and rinse the blender, one or both of my sons will slouch into the kitchen, ask for a sip, and want their own. Now, with a few ingredients and a small blender, they whip up smoothies regularly at school.

1 cup milk (2 percent or nondairy)
2 cups chopped dark leafy greens such as spinach or kale
1 scoop vanilla protein powder
¾ cup frozen mixed berries
1 small banana
1 teaspoon vanilla extract

OPTIONAL ADDITIONS FOR VARIATIONS:
1 tablespoon cocoa powder
1 tablespoon honey
½ cup Greek yogurt (plain or vanilla)
½ avocado
2 tablespoons almond or peanut butter
1 tablespoon chia seeds
1 teaspoon ground cinnamon

Blend the ingredients. Combine the milk, leafy greens, protein powder, berries, banana, vanilla, and any optional additions in a blender and blend until very smooth. Serve.

DORM-FRIENDLY
GLUTEN-FREE

Serves 1

PREP TIME:
5 minutes

BLENDER
MEASURING CUPS
MEASURING SPOONS

PER SERVING
(BASIC RECIPE):
Calories: 411
Fat: 7g
Protein: 37g
Carbohydrates: 54g
Fiber: 7g

Smart Shopping:
Portion the greens, banana, and berries into sealable plastic bags, press the air out, seal, and store in the freezer. Take one out when you make your smoothie and just add your liquids and protein powder.

BERRY-GRANOLA PARFAIT

No matter what your cooking circumstances, you can have a protein-packed breakfast that will keep you satisfied and energized all morning. Creamy yogurt layered with fruit and crunchy granola, and lightly sweetened with maple syrup—it takes about five minutes to throw together and can be a filling snack as well. If you want to use sweetened yogurt, omit the maple syrup.

¼ cup blueberries
¼ cup sliced strawberries
1 cup plain or vanilla Greek yogurt
½ cup granola or chopped pecans
1 tablespoon maple syrup

1 **Combine the berries.** In a small mixing bowl, toss together the blueberries and strawberries.

2 **Layer the parfait.** Spoon half the yogurt into a bowl, top with half the berries and half the granola, and drizzle with half the maple syrup. Repeat with the remaining ingredients.

3 **Serve.**

DORM-FRIENDLY
GLUTEN-FREE

Serves 1

PREP TIME:
5 minutes

MEASURING CUPS
MEASURING SPOONS
SMALL MIXING BOWL
BOWL

PER SERVING:
Calories: 494
Fat: 16g
Protein: 27g
Carbohydrates: 65g
Fiber: 7g

Smart Shopping:
Frozen berries can be as delicious as fresh berries in a dish like this one. Thaw them on paper towels in a container in the refrigerator so they stay intact.

BANANA BREAKFAST CHEESECAKE BOWL

| DORM-FRIENDLY
| GLUTEN-FREE
. . . .
Serves 1
. . . .
PREP TIME:
10 minutes
. . . .
MEASURING CUPS
MEASURING SPOONS
BOWL
. . . .

PER SERVING:
Calories: 872
Fat: 43g
Protein: 34g
Carbohydrates: 96g
Fiber: 7g
. . . .

Variation:
Use different types
of fruit and nuts to
create unique cre-
ations to suit your
palate and pantry
choices.

Ricotta cheese is an underappreciated ingredient with a mild, almost nutty flavor and thick creamy texture that is perfect as a breakfast base. The graham crackers and nuts mimic the traditional crust on a dessert cheesecake, and the banana and maple-flavored cheese base are a decadent combination. This meal will provide about one-fifth of your needed calcium for the day, so your body will thank you.

1 cup part-skim ricotta cheese
2 tablespoons maple syrup
1 large banana, thinly sliced
¼ cup chopped pecans
2 graham crackers, coarsely crushed

1   **Make the bowl.** Spoon the ricotta into a bowl and stir in the maple syrup. Top with banana, pecans, and graham crackers.

2   **Serve.**

NO-BAKE OAT & MAPLE BREAKFAST BARS

These are homemade granola bars that take very little time to create and taste amazing. Store-bought granola bars often have little nutritional value; making your own means controlling the ingredients and no added preservatives.

½ cup peanut butter
2 tablespoons maple syrup
1 teaspoon vanilla extract
½ cup rolled oats
¼ cup shelled sunflower seeds
¼ cup raisins (optional)
2 tablespoons chia seeds

1   **Heat the wet ingredients.** Put the peanut butter, maple syrup, and vanilla in a microwave-safe container and microwave for 20 to 30 seconds on high. Stir to combine.

2   **Mix the bars.** In a medium bowl, stir together the oats, sunflower seeds, raisins (if using), and chia seeds. Add the peanut butter mixture and stir until dough is well mixed and sticks together when pressed.

3   **Form and chill the bars**. Press the mixture into a 6-inch square plastic container or baking dish. Use a knife to partially cut the mixture into 6 (2-by-3-inch) bars. Refrigerate until firm, about 1 hour, and then pop the bars out of the container and cut entirely through.

4   **Store.** Store the bars in a sealed plastic bag in the refrigerator for up to 1 week or in the freezer for 1 month.

DORM-FRIENDLY
GLUTEN-FREE

Serves 2

PREP TIME:
10 minutes, plus
1 hour to chill

COOK TIME:
30 seconds

MEASURING CUPS
MEASURING SPOONS
MEDIUM MIXING
   BOWL
6-INCH SQUARE
   CONTAINER OR
   BAKING DISH
KNIFE

PER SERVING:
Calories: 677
Fat: 47g
Protein: 23g
Carbohydrates: 50g
Fiber: 12g

OVERNIGHT OATS WITH VARIATIONS

| DORM-FRIENDLY

Serves 1

PREP TIME:
5 minutes, plus
overnight soaking
time

MEASURING CUPS
MEASURING SPOONS
CONTAINER OR
   MASON JAR

BASIC:
PER SERVING:
Calories: 268
Fat: 5g
Protein: 9g
Carbohydrates: 47g
Fiber: 4g
PEANUT BUTTER
AND BANANA:
PER SERVING:
Calories: 417
Fat: 14g
Protein: 14g
Carbohydrates: 64g
Fiber: 6g
APPLE PIE:
PER SERVING:
Calories: 410
Fat: 15g
Protein: 11g
Carbohydrates: 62g
Fiber: 8g

The fact you could stir up some oats and liquid and create a delicious porridge was a game-changer for me back when I was in university in the Dark Ages of the '80s. I discovered this by accident when I started making oatmeal on the stove and realized I was late, so I stuck the pot in the fridge and left. When I came home eight hours later, voilà: perfect oatmeal!

FOR BASIC RECIPE
½ cup rolled oats
½ cup milk (2 percent or nondairy)
1 tablespoon maple syrup
1 teaspoon vanilla extract

FOR PEANUT BUTTER AND BANANA
½ banana, sliced
1 tablespoon peanut butter
1 teaspoon chia seeds (optional)

FOR APPLE PIE
½ apple, chopped
2 tablespoons chopped pecans
¼ teaspoon ground cinnamon

FOR CHOCOLATE BROWNIE
1 tablespoon cocoa powder
1 (extra) tablespoon maple syrup
2 tablespoons chocolate chips
1 tablespoon chia seeds (optional)

CHOCOLATE
BROWNIE: PER
SERVING:
Calories: 453
Fat: 13g
Protein: 12g
Carbohydrates: 77g
Fiber: 7g
· · · · · · · · · · · · · · · · ·

1 **Make the overnight oats**. In an airtight container or mason jar, mix the oats, milk, maple syrup, and vanilla. If making a variation, stir in all the other ingredients as well. Seal the container and let soak overnight in the refrigerator.

2 **Serve.** Stir the oats and serve.

CINNAMON COFFEE CAKE

DORM-FRIENDLY

Serves 1

PREP TIME:
5 minutes

COOK TIME:
1 minute 30 seconds

MICROWAVE
MEASURING CUPS
MEASURING SPOONS
LARGE MUG
SMALL MIXING BOWL

PER SERVING:
Calories: 415
Fat: 21g
Protein: 10g
Carbohydrates: 47g
Fiber: 1g

This is basically a fluffy, cinnamon-scented, single-serve muffin, but it has all the elements of a bakery cake. You will want to purchase a deep, wide coffee mug with a big handle to make mug recipes like this one. If you want a real coffee cake experience, mix the batter and topping in separate bowls and layer half the batter, then half the topping, and repeat.

FOR THE CAKE
¼ cup all-purpose flour
1 tablespoon brown sugar
¼ teaspoon baking powder
1 large egg
1 tablespoon melted butter or canola oil
½ teaspoon vanilla

FOR THE TOPPING
1 tablespoon brown sugar
½ tablespoon all-purpose flour
¼ teaspoon ground cinnamon
Pinch salt
1 teaspoon soft butter

1   **Mix the cake.** In a large mug, stir together the flour, brown sugar, and baking powder. Add the egg, butter, and vanilla and stir until combined.

2   **Make the topping.** In a small bowl, stir together the brown sugar, flour, cinnamon, salt, and butter until the mixture resembles coarse crumbs.

3   **Top and cook.** Sprinkle the topping on the cake batter and micro-wave 1 minute to 90 seconds, until cooked through and fluffy.

4   **Serve.** Let cool for 5 minutes and serve.

BANANA FRENCH TOAST

DORM-FRIENDLY

Serves 1

PREP TIME:
5 minutes, plus
5 minutes soaking
time

COOK TIME:
1 minute 30 seconds

MICROWAVE
MEASURING CUPS
MEASURING SPOONS
MEDIUM MIXING
   BOWL
WHISK
LARGE MUG OR
   8-OUNCE RAMEKIN

PER SERVING:
Calories: 471
Fat: 18g
Protein: 19g
Carbohydrates: 62g
Fiber: 12g

Variation:
Replace the banana
with chopped
pecans, blueberries,
or chocolate chips.

Who knew you could make delectable French toast in the microwave in less than 15 minutes? No skillet or supervision is required! Adding sweet banana means no topping is necessary, and you can enjoy this dish warm or cold, depending on your schedule.

2 teaspoons salted butter
¼ cup milk (2 percent or nondairy)
1 large egg
¼ teaspoon vanilla extract
2 thick slices multigrain bread, cut into 1-inch cubes
½ banana, sliced

OPTIONAL TOPPINGS
Syrup
Chocolate chips
Whipped cream

1 **Melt the butter.** Put the butter in a large mug and microwave for 5 seconds to melt.

2 **Soak the bread.** In a medium bowl, whisk the milk, egg, and vanilla until well blended. Add the bread cubes and banana slices and toss to coat. Let stand for 5 minutes to soak.

3 **Microwave.** Transfer the bread to the mug and microwave for 1 minute and 10 seconds, or until the egg is cooked.

4 **Serve.** Serve the French toast with your favorite toppings.

OATMEAL-CINNAMON PANCAKES

Pancakes might seem like a less-than-optimal nutrition choice, but when you add oatmeal, the fiber content increases, so you will feel full no matter how busy your day is.

½ cup all-purpose flour
⅓ cup rolled oats
1 teaspoon baking powder
¾ cup milk (2 percent or nondairy), at room temperature
1 large egg, at room temperature
1 teaspoon melted butter or canola oil
1 teaspoon vanilla extract
Nonstick cooking spray
Syrup for serving

1 **Make the batter.** In a medium bowl, stir together the flour, oats, and baking powder until blended. Make a well in the center and pour in the milk, egg, butter, and vanilla. Stir until just mixed.

2 **Cook the pancakes.** Heat a large skillet on a stovetop or hot plate on medium-high heat. Lightly spray the skillet with cooking spray and scoop the pancake batter in ¼-cup measures into the skillet. Cook until the edges are golden and firm, about 3 minutes. Flip and cook until both sides are golden, and the center is cooked, about 2 minutes more. Transfer the pancakes to a plate and repeat with the remaining batter.

3 **Serve.** Top with your favorite syrup and serve.

Serves 1

PREP TIME:
7 minutes

COOK TIME:
10 minutes

STOVETOP OR HOT PLATE
MEASURING CUPS
MEASURING SPOONS
MEDIUM MIXING BOWL
LARGE SKILLET
SPATULA

PER SERVING:
Calories: 537
Fat: 15g
Protein: 22g
Carbohydrates: 77g
Fiber: 5g

Dorm Hack:
Lightly grease an 8-ounce ramekin, scoop in a ¼ cup measure of batter, and microwave for 1 minute. Pop out the pancake, then regrease the ramekin, repeat, and serve with syrup.

WESTERN OMELET IN A MUG

DORM-FRIENDLY
GLUTEN-FREE

. . . .

Serves 1

. . . .

PREP TIME:
5 minutes

. . . .

COOK TIME:
3 minutes

. . . .

MICROWAVE
MEASURING CUPS
KNIFE
CUTTING BOARD
LARGE MUG
   OR 8-OUNCE
   RAMEKIN

. . . .

PER SERVING:
Calories: 386
Fat: 23g
Protein: 32g
Carbohydrates: 14g
Fiber: 1g

. . . .

My 18-year-old son spends more time trying to convince me to cook breakfast for him than the time it would take him to make this simple egg dish. When I walked him through it, he just grinned and started making his own variations a couple times a week. When he went off for the in-class part of his apprenticeship, this recipe became a speedy grab-and-go breakfast when wrapped in a tortilla.

2 large eggs
¼ cup milk
Sea salt
Ground black pepper
¼ cup shredded cheese (cheddar, Swiss, Gouda)
¼ red bell pepper, chopped
2 tablespoons chopped red onion
1 slice ham or cooked bacon, chopped

1 **Beat the eggs.** Crack the eggs into the mug and stir in the milk until well blended. Season with salt and pepper.

2 **Add the other ingredients**. Stir in the cheese, bell pepper, onion, and ham until combined.

3 **Cook the omelet.** Cover the mug with a paper towel and microwave on high for 2½ to 3 minutes, or until fully cooked.

4 **Serve.** Add fresh fruit or sliced tomato for a more complete meal.

BREAKFAST NACHOS

Nachos for breakfast—wait, what? Okay, while these are not *real* nachos with heaps of ground beef and cheese, they look just as tantalizing and have many of the same essential ingredients.

1 tablespoon butter or canola oil
½ red bell pepper, chopped
¼ sweet or red onion, chopped
4 large eggs
Tortilla chips, for serving
1 cup canned beans, drained and rinsed
½ cup store-bought salsa
½ cup shredded cheddar cheese
½ avocado, chopped (optional)

1 **Cook the veggies.** Heat the butter in a small skillet over medium-high heat on a stovetop or hot plate. Add the red pepper and onion, and sauté until the veggies are softened, about 3 minutes.

2 **Cook the eggs.** In a small bowl, beat the eggs and then pour them into the skillet. Scramble with the veggies by repeatedly drawing a spatula across the skillet to move the cooked eggs. Scramble until the eggs form fluffy curds that are cooked through but still moist, about 2 minutes. Remove from the heat.

3 **Make the nachos.** Arrange the tortilla chips on a plate and top with the scrambled eggs, beans, salsa, cheddar, and avocado (if using).

4 **Serve.**

GLUTEN-FREE

Serves 2

PREP TIME:
10 minutes

COOK TIME:
5 minutes

STOVETOP OR HOT PLATE
MEASURING CUPS
MEASURING SPOONS
SMALL BOWL
SKILLET
SPATULA
CAN OPENER

PER SERVING:
Calories: 449
Fat: 27g
Protein: 27g
Carbohydrates: 27g
Fiber: 7g

Dorm Hack:
Microwave the veggies for 1 minute 30 seconds, add the eggs, and microwave for another minute. Continue with the recipe as written.

HUEVOS RANCHEROS WRAPS

| GLUTEN-FREE

Serves 1

PREP TIME:
10 minutes

COOK TIME:
1 minute 30 seconds

STOVETOP OR HOT
    PLATE
MEASURING CUPS
MEASURING SPOONS
SMALL MIXING BOWL
SKILLET
WHISK
SPATULA
CAN OPENER

PER SERVING:
Calories: 566
Fat: 33g
Protein: 28g
Carbohydrates: 43g
Fiber: 12g

Huevos rancheros is a dish of Mexican origin that features salsa, beans, tortillas, and eggs. This version is a hearty, flavorful combination that is folded into a tortilla to form a handy wrap.

1 teaspoon butter
2 large eggs, lightly beaten
Sea salt
Ground black pepper
2 (6-inch) corn tortillas
2 tablespoons guacamole, store-bought or homemade (see page 128)
¼ cup store-bought or homemade salsa
¼ cup canned black beans, drained and rinsed
¼ cup shredded cheddar cheese

OPTIONAL GARNISH:
1 teaspoon chopped fresh cilantro or ½ teaspoon dried
1 lime, quartered

1 **Melt the butter.** Melt the butter in a small skillet placed over medium-high heat on a stovetop or hot plate.

2 **Beat the eggs.** In a small bowl, beat the eggs with salt and pepper.

3 **Cook the eggs.** Pour the eggs into the skillet and scramble until moist but completely cooked by repeatedly drawing a spatula across the skillet and scraping up the cooked egg in fluffy curds. Remove from the heat.

4   **Arrange the wraps**. Place the tortillas on a clean surface and evenly divide the eggs between them. Top with the guacamole, salsa, black beans, cheddar, and cilantro (if using).

5   **Serve.** Roll the tortillas up and serve with lime wedges (if using).

GRAB-AND-GO BREAKFAST SANDWICHES

DORM-FRIENDLY

Serves 1

PREP TIME:
10 minutes

COOK TIME:
1 minute

MICROWAVE
TOASTER, OPTIONAL
SMALL MIXING BOWL
6-OUNCE RAMEKIN

PER SERVING:
Calories: 444
Fat: 24g
Protein: 28g
Carbohydrates: 27g
Fiber: 2g

Breakfast sandwiches are the drive-through choice for both my kids— on English muffins, biscuits, and even waffles. They get three at a time, and the sandwiches are often gone before we pull out of the line after paying. Making these at home is much more cost-effective, and they can still swap out the muffins for a warm toaster-waffle base.

2 large eggs
Sea salt
Ground black pepper
Nonstick cooking spray
1 English muffin, split and toasted, if possible
2 pieces cooked bacon or ham, or 1 precooked sausage patty
1 slice cheese (Cheddar, Swiss, Monterey Jack)
1 tomato slice (optional)

1 **Beat the eggs.** In a small bowl, whisk the eggs and season with salt and pepper.

2 **Cook the eggs.** Lightly spray a 6-ounce ramekin with cooking spray and pour in the eggs. Microwave uncovered for 30 seconds on high, stir, and microwave in 10-second intervals until the eggs are set, about 30 seconds more.

3   **Arrange the sandwich.** Place the English muffin halves on a clean work surface and arrange the meat on the bottom half. Run a knife around the inside of the ramekin to release the egg and place the egg on the meat. Top with cheese and tomato (if using).

4   **Serve.**

Love Your Leftovers: The completed sandwich can be cooled, put in a sealed plastic bag, and frozen for up to 1 month. To reheat, wrap the sandwich in paper towels and microwave in 30-second intervals until warmed through.

BISTRO CHICKEN CAESAR SANDWICH, PAGE 48

CHAPTER THREE
SALADS *AND* SANDWICHES

MASTERING THE BASICS: MASON JAR SALAD

Mason jar salads can be a game-changer for college meals, especially because they are packed with healthy ingredients and usually several servings of veggies. How long you can keep your salads in the refrigerator depends on what you stuff into the jars. If the jar is just veggies and dressing, expect at least a week. If the salad contains meats, poultry, or cheese, then five days is the limit. Cut fruit will change that refrigeration time to three days. Pack the salads in the following order, bottom to top. You can use or omit any of the layers to your liking, except for the dressing and greens.

DRESSING: Put this component at the bottom to keep the lettuce and other ingredients crisp and fresh. Use 2 to 3 tablespoons of whatever dressing you'd like.

HARD VEGGIES OR FRUIT: Add a few pieces of cooked baby or cut potatoes, carrots, cooked parsnips, celery, or cooked corn.

GRAINS OR LEGUMES: Add about ¼ cup cooked rice, quinoa, bulgur, chickpeas, black beans, pasta, or lentils.

PROTEIN: Layer in cooked chicken, beef, turkey, tofu, pork, hard-boiled eggs, or canned tuna.

SOFT VEGGIES, FRUIT, NUTS, AND SEEDS: Layer in berries, cherries, asparagus, red pepper, cherry tomatoes, sunflower seeds, almonds, pecans, or pistachios.

GREENS: This layer should be ⅓ to ½ of the jar. Try mixed greens, spinach, or kale.

STRAWBERRY-NUT SALAD

Everyone seems to have a recipe for this type of salad, but don't let that fool you into thinking it is ordinary. These copious culinary tributes to greens, strawberries, nuts, and cheese are so popular because the combination is exceptional. The colors and textures on the plate will remind you of summer: fresh and bright.

2 cups chopped romaine, baby spinach, or baby greens

1 cup sliced fresh strawberries

⅛ small red onion, thinly sliced

3 tablespoons store-bought dressing, such as balsamic vinaigrette, divided

¼ cup chopped nuts, such as pecans or almonds

¼ cup crumbled goat cheese or feta

2 tablespoons dried cranberries

2 tablespoons roasted sunflower seeds

¼ chopped avocado (optional)

1 **Dress the salad.** Combine the greens, strawberries, and onion in a medium bowl and toss with 2 tablespoons of dressing.

2 **Top the salad.** Arrange the salad on a large plate and top with the nuts, cheese, cranberries, sunflower seeds, and avocado (if using). Drizzle with the remaining dressing.

3 **Serve.**

| DORM-FRIENDLY
| GLUTEN-FREE
. . . .
Serves 1
. . . .
PREP TIME:
15 minutes
. . . .
MEDIUM MIXING
  BOWL
MEASURING CUPS
MEASURING SPOONS
KNIFE
CUTTING BOARD
. . . .
PER SERVING:
Calories: 669
Fat: 52g
Protein: 14g
Carbohydrates: 44g
Fiber: 10g
. . . .

Make It Yourself:
You can easily make balsamic dressing by mixing ¼ cup oil, 2 tablespoons balsamic vinegar, 1 teaspoon honey, 1 teaspoon mustard, and a pinch each of salt and pepper.

CHICKEN MANDARIN SALAD

| DORM-FRIENDLY

Serves 2

PREP TIME:
15 minutes

MEDIUM MIXING
  BOWL
MEASURING CUPS
MEASURING SPOONS
BOX GRATER
KNIFE
CUTTING BOARD
CAN OPENER

PER SERVING:
Calories: 547
Fat: 23g
Protein: 49g
Carbohydrates: 35g
Fiber: 13g

Looking for a comforting but exciting meal choice for a filling lunch or light dinner? This salad is a gorgeous no-cook option and big enough to share with a friend or have leftovers for another meal. If you want a vegetarian option or don't have chicken handy, it is still delicious without meat.

1 (10-ounce) bag of shredded cabbage

2 cups shredded lettuce

2 cups shredded cooked chicken or 2 (5-ounce) cans no-salt-added chicken, drained

1 (8-ounce) can mandarin oranges packed in juice, drained

1 carrot, shredded

½ cup sliced almonds

2 teaspoons chopped fresh cilantro, or 1 teaspoon dried (optional)

½ cup store-bought tahini dressing

Smart Shopping:
To save chopping time, you can substitute 2 (10-ounce) bags of coleslaw mix in place of the shredded lettuce, cabbage, and carrot.

1   **Make the salad.** In a medium bowl, toss together the cabbage, lettuce, chicken, oranges, carrot, almonds, and cilantro (if using) until well mixed.

2   **Dress the salad.** Add the dressing and toss until the salad is well coated.

3   **Serve.**

VEGETARIAN TACO BOWL

You might be familiar with bowls from your favorite trendy restaurant and can create your own to take on the go using the sidebar on page 78. This version has a Southwest theme and is inspired by vegetarian tacos with a soy crumble base. This is the ideal meal to put together on a study break away from any screens.

1 cup soy crumbles
1 tablespoon taco seasoning
4 cups shredded romaine lettuce
1 cup canned black beans, drained and rinsed
1 cup frozen or canned corn, drained and rinsed
2 large tomatoes, seeded and diced
¼ cup pickled jalapeño peppers
¼ cup sour cream (optional)
¼ cup crushed tortilla chips

1. **Heat the soy crumbles.** Put the soy crumbles in a microwave-safe dish and add 2 tablespoons of water and the taco seasoning. Microwave for 1 minute on high.

2. **Make the bowls.** Divide the lettuce between 2 bowls and top with the soy crumbles, beans, corn, tomatoes, jalapeños, sour cream (if using), and tortilla chips.

3. **Serve.**

DORM-FRIENDLY
GLUTEN-FREE
. . . .
Serves 2
. . . .
PREP TIME:
15 minutes
. . . .
COOK TIME:
1 minute
. . . .
MICROWAVE
SMALL MICROWAVE-
   SAFE BOWL
MEASURING CUPS
MEASURING SPOONS
KNIFE
CUTTING BOARD
CAN OPENER
. . . .
PER SERVING:
Calories: 361
Fat: 5g
Protein: 26g
Carbohydrates: 67g
Fiber: 20g
. . . .

MEDITERRANEAN COUSCOUS SALAD

Couscous looks like a grain, but it is actually a pasta, made of little balls of semolina durum wheat that has been steamed and dried. This ingredient is perfect for college cooking because it only takes a bit of hot water and about 10 minutes sitting time to cook. Then you just fluff the couscous, mix with whatever you want, and enjoy! This salad combines tender couscous with all the flavors and textures of a fresh Greek salad.

1 cup dry couscous
1 medium cucumber, chopped
1 cup halved cherry tomatoes
1 bell pepper (any color), chopped
¼ red onion, chopped
¼ cup sliced olives
½ cup crumbled feta cheese
2 tablespoons chopped fresh parsley or 1 tablespoon dried (optional)
½ cup store-bought balsamic dressing
lemon wedges, for garnishing

1 **Make the couscous.** Put the couscous in a medium bowl and use an electric kettle to boil 2 cups of water. Pour the water into the couscous and set aside for 10 minutes, then fluff with a fork.

2 **Make the salad.** Add the cucumber, tomatoes, bell pepper, onion, olives, feta, parsley, and dressing, and toss to mix.

3 **Serve.** Garnish with lemon wedges and serve hot.

DORM-FRIENDLY

Serves 2

PREP TIME:
15 minutes

COOK TIME:
2 minutes

ELECTRIC KETTLE
MEASURING CUPS
MEASURING SPOONS
MEDIUM MIXING
    BOWL
KNIFE
CUTTING BOARD

PER SERVING:
Calories: 718
Fat: 33g
Protein: 19g
Carbohydrates: 88g
Fiber: 8g

Variation:
You can use quinoa, rice, or cooked pasta in the same amount instead of couscous.

CAULIFLOWER RICE SALAD

GLUTEN-FREE
. . . .
Serves 2
. . . .
PREP TIME:
6 minutes
. . . .
COOK TIME:
14 minutes
. . . .
STOVETOP OR HOT
   PLATE
MEASURING CUPS
MEASURING SPOONS
MEDIUM MIXING
   BOWL
LARGE SKILLET
SPATULA
. . . .
PER SERVING:
Calories: 249
Fat: 13g
Protein: 14g
Carbohydrates: 21g
Fiber: 7g
. . . .

If you are a fan of takeout fried rice, this cauliflower version will be a real treat. Use the recipe as a base for your own fabulous variations, adding chicken, shrimp, or more vegetables. You can heat the cauliflower and other ingredients—except the eggs—in the microwave on high for 30-second intervals until softened, about three minutes in total, but you won't get the yummy, lightly browned edges.

1 small head cauliflower or 1 (12-ounce) package cauliflower rice

1 tablespoon sesame oil

1 carrot, chopped

2 scallions, chopped

1 teaspoon minced garlic

1 teaspoon minced ginger

1 cup frozen peas

1 ½ tablespoons soy sauce

2 large eggs

1. **Prep the cauliflower.** If using a whole head, finely chop the cauliflower.

2. **Cook the rice.** Heat the oil in a large skillet on a stovetop or hot plate on medium-high heat. Add the cauliflower, carrot, scallions, garlic, and ginger, and sauté until softened and lightly browned, about 10 minutes. Add the peas and soy sauce and sauté 2 minutes more.

3. **Add the eggs.** Push the cauliflower rice to one side and pour the eggs into the skillet. Scramble the eggs by repeatedly drawing a spatula across the skillet to create fluffy, moist curds, about 2 minutes. Stir the cooked egg into the rice.

4. **Serve.**

BISTRO CHICKEN CAESAR SANDWICH

DORM-FRIENDLY

Serves 1

PREP TIME:
10 minutes

MEASURING SPOONS

PER SERVING:
Calories: 518
Fat: 23g
Protein: 41g
Carbohydrates: 36g
Fiber: 2g

Love Your Leftovers:
If you buy a standard 8.8-ounce package of precooked chicken, you will have half left over for other recipes. Try it in the Homestyle Chicken Alphabet Soup (page 65).

My boys love Caesar salads, so a sandwich with all those wonderful flavors is a favorite lunch or dinner choice. We often use tortillas instead of buns to create this dish. This recipe is made with convenient store-bought chicken breast, bacon, and dressing to save time. You can certainly cook the chicken yourself, as well as the bacon, but the premade products are fuss-free and generally inexpensive.

1 large crusty bun, halved lengthwise
2 tablespoons store-bought Caesar dressing
4 ounces store-bought cooked chicken breast, sliced
3 slices store-bought cooked bacon (optional)
2 large lettuce leaves

1 **Make the sandwich.** Spread the Caesar dressing on both sides of the bun. Pile the chicken, bacon (if using), and lettuce on the bottom bun and top with the other half.

2 **Serve.**

STACKED GRILLED CHEESE SANDWICH

Have you ever had a three-layer sandwich at a restaurant and thought it looked complicated? I promise it is not, and this recipe will prove it. If you want a heartier version, add cooked chicken or bacon.

3 slices of your favorite bread
1 tablespoon butter
4 (1-ounce) slices cheddar or Swiss cheese
1 tomato, thinly sliced
½ avocado, thinly sliced

1 **Arrange the sandwiches.** Butter 1 side of each slice of the bread. Place 2 slices of cheese on the unbuttered sides of 2 pieces of the bread. Arrange the tomato slices and avocado on the unbuttered side of the third slice of bread.

2 **Brown the bread.** Place a large skillet on a stovetop or hot plate on medium heat. Place the slices butter-side down in the skillet. Cook until the bread is golden brown, and the cheese is melted, 3 to 4 minutes.

3 **Arrange the sandwich.** Remove the skillet from the heat and use a spatula to place one of the cheese-covered slices golden-side down on a plate. Top with the tomato-and-avocado-topped slice, golden-side down. Top the sandwich with the third slice, cheese-side down.

4 **Serve.**

Serves 1

PREP TIME:
10 minutes

COOK TIME:
3 minutes

STOVETOP OR HOT PLATE
MEASURING SPOONS
LARGE SKILLET
SPATULA

PER SERVING:
Calories: 1054
Fat: 66g
Protein: 44g
Carbohydrates: 81g
Fiber: 21g

Smart Shopping:
If you don't have any butter, you can also use mayonnaise!

CHICKEN SALAD WRAPS

Chicken salad is a staple for many college students because it can be a topping or eaten on its own. What is not to like about tender chicken, crunchy veggies, creamy mayo, and a hint of citrus?

| DORM-FRIENDLY

Serves 2

PREP TIME:
15 minutes

MEDIUM MIXING BOWL
MEASURING CUPS
MEASURING SPOONS
KNIFE
CUTTING BOARD

PER SERVING:
Calories: 437
Fat: 25g
Protein: 22g
Carbohydrates: 29g
Fiber: 1g

Smart Shopping: Buy a rotisserie chicken, chill, and remove the meat, discarding the skin. Portion the chicken into 1-cup measures, then store in the refrigerator for up to 3 days and the freezer for up to 1 month.

1 cup diced cooked chicken or 1 (5-ounce) can no-salt-added chicken, drained
1 celery stalk, chopped
¼ red bell pepper, chopped
2 tablespoons chopped onion
¼ cup mayonnaise
1 tablespoon lime juice
Salt
Ground black pepper
2 (8- to 10-inch) flour or corn tortillas
½ cup shredded lettuce

1 **Make the chicken salad.** In a large bowl, combine the chicken, celery, bell pepper, onion, mayonnaise, and lime juice until mixed. Season with salt and pepper.

2 **Roll up the wraps.** Place the tortillas on a clean work surface and divide the chicken mixture between them. Top with the shredded lettuce. Take 1 tortilla, fold opposite sides over the filling, and then roll the wrap, starting from the unfolded end closest to you. Repeat with the other tortilla.

3 **Serve.**

CHICKPEA SALAD ON TOAST

Legumes provide heaps of protein, complex carbs, iron, and vitamin B to your diet, all of which are crucial for managing stress and sustaining energy. This recipe is the vegetarian version of meat-based salads but it is equally satisfying and delicious.

1 (15-ounce) can no-sodium-added chickpeas, drained and rinsed
¼ cup mayonnaise
½ lemon, juiced
1 teaspoon sriracha sauce (optional)
Salt
Ground black pepper
¼ small sweet onion, chopped
1 teaspoon chopped fresh cilantro or ½ teaspoon dried (optional)
4 slices of your favorite bread
1 tablespoon butter (optional)

1 **Make the chickpea salad.** Put the chickpeas in a medium bowl and mash them with a fork until a coarse paste is formed. Stir in the mayonnaise, lemon juice, and sriracha (if using) until well mixed. Season with salt and pepper. Stir in the onion and cilantro.

2 **Make the sandwiches.** Toast the bread in a toaster, spread the butter onto the toast (if using), and evenly divide the chickpea mixture between the toast slices.

3 **Serve.**

DORM-FRIENDLY

Serves 2

PREP TIME:
15 minutes

COOK TIME:
3 minutes

TOASTER
MICROWAVE
MEASURING CUPS
MEASURING SPOONS
MEDIUM MIXING
   BOWL
CAN OPENER
KNIFE
CUTTING BOARD

PER SERVING:
Calories: 698
Fat: 40g
Protein: 54g
Carbohydrates: 28g
Fiber: 3g

HEARTY TUNA ENGLISH MUFFIN MELTS

Serves 2

PREP TIME:
15 minutes

COOK TIME:
3 minutes

TOASTER
MICROWAVE
MEASURING CUPS
MEASURING SPOONS
MEDIUM MIXING
   BOWL
CAN OPENER
KNIFE
CUTTING BOARD

PER SERVING:
Calories: 698
Fat: 40g
Protein: 54g
Carbohydrates: 28g
Fiber: 3g

Is there a diner anywhere in North America without some sort of tuna melt on the menu? This sandwich is undeniably flavorful, and you feel satisfied after eating it. The dill pickles and hot peppers add a boost to the traditional tuna and mayo salad.

2 (5-ounce) cans water-packed tuna
¼ small red onion, chopped
1 celery stalk, chopped
2 tablespoons chopped dill pickles
1 tablespoon chopped pickled jalapeño peppers (optional)
¼ cup mayonnaise
1 teaspoon mustard
Sea salt
Ground black pepper
2 English muffins
4 (1-ounce) cheese slices (Swiss or cheddar)

1 **Make the tuna salad.** In a medium bowl, combine the tuna, onion, celery, pickles, jalapeños (if using), mayonnaise, and mustard. Season lightly with salt and pepper.

2 **Put the melts together.** Toast the English muffin halves and place them on a clean work surface. Evenly divide the tuna mixture between the muffin halves and top each with a cheese slice.

3 **Melt the cheese.** Place the halves on a paper towel in the microwave and microwave on high until the cheese is melted, about 30 seconds.

4 **Serve.**

MINI PITA-POCKET PIZZAS

DORM-FRIENDLY
. . . .
Serves 1
. . . .
PREP TIME:
10 minutes
. . . .
COOK TIME:
2 minutes
. . . .
TOASTER OVEN
MEASURING CUPS
MEASURING SPOONS
KNIFE
CUTTING BOARD
. . . .
PER SERVING:
Calories: 464
Fat: 28g
Protein: 35g
Carbohydrates: 26g
Fiber: 7g
. . . .

My youngest loves pizza pockets; he would eat them every day if they weren't bad for him. I created this recipe on a day when I had not replenished his supply, but he had a craving. I walked into the kitchen to behold a smug young man popping DIY pockets out of my toaster oven. We now use the same method to make scrambled egg and cheese breakfast pockets and even s'mores pockets filled with chocolate spread, mini marshmallows, and banana slices.

2 mini whole-wheat pita breads
¼ cup store-bought pizza sauce
¾ cup shredded mozzarella cheese

OPTIONAL FILLINGS
5 pepperoni slices
1 (1-ounce) slice ham, chopped
2 slices bacon, chopped
2 mushrooms, sliced
4 olives, sliced
4 pickled jalapeño pepper slices
2 tomato slices
1 tablespoon shredded fresh basil

1 **Stuff the pocket.** Carefully cut the pita tops open about three inches, just enough so you can stuff the pocket. Evenly divide the sauce between the pitas, spreading it on the inside of each one. Sprinkle in the cheese, pressing it against the sauce. Add whatever fillings you wish, being careful not to fill them too full.

2 **Cook the pita pockets.** Place the pitas, cut-side up, in the toaster oven and toast on a medium setting, about 2 minutes.

3 **Serve.** Carefully remove the pockets from the toaster oven and serve.

COBB LETTUCE WRAPS

DORM-FRIENDLY

GLUTEN-FREE
. . . .
Serves 2
. . . .
PREP TIME:
15 minutes
. . . .
MEDIUM MIXING
    BOWL
MEASURING CUPS
KNIFE
CUTTING BOARD
. . . .
PER SERVING:
Calories: 356
Fat: 25g
Protein: 27g
Carbohydrates: 4g
Fiber: 1g
. . . .

Cobb salad is famous, created at the Brown Derby restaurant in California in 1937. Eating this salad-inspired wrap means you are now part of a long culinary history. You can turn this into an actual salad by chopping up the lettuce leaves. Or create a grab-and-go meal by wrapping all the ingredients in a tortilla or stuffing them in a pita half.

1 cup chopped cooked chicken or 1 (5-ounce) can no-salt-added chicken, drained

2 bacon slices, chopped

1 hard-boiled egg, chopped

1 small tomato, chopped

½ avocado, chopped (optional)

¼ cup crumbled blue or feta cheese

¼ cup store-bought ranch dressing

4 large iceberg lettuce leaves

1 **Make the filling.** In a medium bowl, stir together the chicken, bacon, egg, tomato, avocado (if using), cheese, and dressing until mixed.

2 **Make the wraps.** Evenly divide the filling among the lettuce leaves.

3 **Serve.**

Smart Shopping:
Cooked bacon can be bought as slices or bits, depending on your needs; there are about 12 slices per package. They can be kept in the pantry instead of the refrigerator if you put them in sealed plastic bags after opening the package.

SOUPS
AND STEWS

MASTERING THE BASICS: RAMEN

Ramen: the unofficial food mascot of almost every college. It is tasty, inexpensive, speedy, and requires only a kettle or microwave to cook. So why mess with perfection? Well, that handy flavor pouch can contain upwards of 1,800 mg of sodium, or almost 90 percent of your daily allotment. If you want to enjoy the convenience of ramen without the risk of bloating—and you can!—try doctoring those packages as I've outlined below:

1. CHANGE THE BROTH: Use 2 cups of low-sodium veggie or chicken broth instead of water plus the seasoning packet. Perk up the broth with coconut milk, a tablespoon of peanut butter, sriracha sauce, sesame oil, miso, hoisin sauce, garlic, or ginger.

2. ADD VEGGIES: Almost any veggie can be added to ramen if you slice it thinly so the cooking time isn't affected. If you are simmering your ramen on a stovetop or hot plate, simply add the veggies with the noodles. Try carrots, bell pepper, mushrooms, broccoli, peas, spinach, kale, or cabbage.

3. ADD PROTEIN: You can make ramen a satisfying meal by adding chopped chicken, pork, shrimp, fish, tofu, tempeh, or a hard-boiled egg. Use fully cooked proteins you can reheat instead of cook, to avoid food safety issues.

4. ADD TOPPINGS: Ramen has ample room for more flavor and texture. Try crispy chow mein noodles, sesame seeds, chopped scallion or cilantro, nori (dried seaweed wrap), or lime wedges.

VEGGIE RAMEN NOODLE SOUP

You would need to duck to avoid the avalanche of badly stacked ramen packages that tumble out of the kitchen cupboards at both my sons' apartments. I lived on this staple during my own university years, but I like this dressed-up ramen because I know exactly what's in it.

1 (3-ounce) package ramen noodles
1 (12-ounce) package broccoli slaw or coleslaw mix
½ cup thinly sliced white mushrooms (optional)
2 teaspoons low-sodium vegetable or chicken bouillon
1 tablespoon low-sodium soy sauce
1 tablespoon sriracha sauce
4 cups boiling water

1 **Cook the ramen.** Place the saucepan filled three-quarters full of water over high heat and bring to a boil. Add the ramen noodles and cook according to the package instructions, about 5 minutes. Drain noodles in a colander, then run cold water over them.

2 **Layer the ingredients.** Evenly divide the ingredients between 2 sealable containers (or mason jars) in the following order: cooked ramen noodles, slaw, mushrooms (if using), bouillon, soy sauce, and sriracha. Seal and place in the refrigerator for up to 2 days.

3 **Serve.** Take a container out of the refrigerator, add 2 cups of boiling water, and let stand for 5 minutes, stirring once.

Serves 2

PREP TIME:
5 minutes

COOK TIME:
5 minutes

STOVETOP OR HOT
  PLATE
MEDIUM SAUCEPAN
MEASURING CUPS
MEASURING SPOONS
COLANDER
2 (4-CUP) SEALABLE
  CONTAINERS OR
  MASON JARS

PER SERVING:
Calories: 233
Fat: 7g
Protein: 9g
Carbohydrates: 35g
Fiber: 5g

Dorm Hack:
Microwave 2 cups of water for 3 minutes, add noodles, and microwave for another 5. Continue the recipe at step 2.

CREAMY PUMPKIN SOUP

Pumpkin in soup? But pumpkin is for pies and for carving funny faces in at Halloween! Think again about your favorite orange squash because this ingredient can be used in casseroles, stews, and this warm, spiced soup. Canned pumpkin makes preparation a breeze and gives the soup a luscious, velvety texture. Make sure you get pure pumpkin, not pie filling, which has added sugar and spices.

1 cup vegetable broth
1 cup canned pumpkin
¼ cup heavy (whipping) cream
2 tablespoons maple syrup
¼ teaspoon onion powder
¼ teaspoon ground cinnamon
⅛ teaspoon ground ginger
⅛ teaspoon ground nutmeg
Sea salt
Ground black pepper
Roasted pepitas, for garnishing (optional)

1 **Combine the ingredients.** In a medium saucepan, whisk together the vegetable broth, pumpkin, cream, maple syrup, onion powder, cinnamon, ginger, and nutmeg.

CONTINUED ▶

GLUTEN-FREE

Serves 2

PREP TIME:
2 minutes

COOK TIME:
14 minutes

STOVETOP OR HOT PLATE
MEDIUM SAUCEPAN
MEASURING CUPS
MEASURING SPOONS
WHISK
CAN OPENER

PER SERVING:
Calories: 200
Fat: 11g
Protein: 3g
Carbohydrates: 25g
Fiber: 4g

Love Your Leftovers:
The leftover pumpkin from the can be thrown into smoothies, spaghetti sauce, or baked into a dessert.

2   **Cook the soup.** Place the saucepan over medium-high heat and cook until the soup just comes to a boil, about 4 minutes. Reduce the heat to low and simmer the soup, stirring occasionally, for 10 minutes.

3   **Serve.** Season with salt and pepper, garnish with pepitas (if using), and serve.

HOMESTYLE CHICKEN ALPHABET SOUP

Alphabet soup was a family favorite for lunch when the kids were young because we spent most of the meal spelling out names and sentences on plates and spoons. My sons don't fish letters out of their soup anymore, but this recipe is still a popular choice. Alphabet pasta is the perfect size and thickness to cook in the microwave, but you can also use fine egg noodles made specially for soup.

1 cup low-sodium chicken broth
½ cup shredded cooked or canned chicken, drained
1 small carrot, peeled, halved lengthwise, and sliced
1 scallion, both white and green parts, sliced
2 tablespoons dried alphabet pasta
Sea salt
Ground black pepper
Sprinkle of dried parsley (optional)

1 **Combine the ingredients.** In the large mug, stir together the broth, chicken, carrot, scallion, and pasta.

2 **Cook the soup.** Cover the mug with a plastic microwave shield and microwave on high heat for 6 minutes, stirring halfway through, until the noodles are tender, and the soup is piping hot.

3 **Serve.** Season with salt, pepper, and parsley (if using).

DORM-FRIENDLY

Serves 1

PREP TIME:
5 minutes

COOK TIME:
6 minutes

MICROWAVE
LARGE (16-OUNCE) MUG
MEASURING CUPS
MEASURING SPOONS
KNIFE
CUTTING BOARD

PER SERVING:
Calories: 259
Fat: 4g
Protein: 27g
Carbohydrates: 28g
Fiber: 3g

Love Your Leftovers:
Alphabet pasta is fun and tasty in soups and tossed with tomato sauce or pesto.

EGG DROP SOUP

Egg drop soup is created when you slowly drizzle beaten egg into simmering broth, creating tender cooked-egg ribbons. While it is common at Chinese restaurants, you can easily make your own.

GLUTEN-FREE

. . . .

Serves 2

. . . .

PREP TIME:
5 minutes

. . . .

COOK TIME:
10 minutes

. . . .

STOVETOP OR HOT
  PLATE
MEDIUM SAUCEPAN
MEASURING CUPS
MEASURING SPOONS
2 SMALL MIXING
  BOWLS
KNIFE
CUTTING BOARD

. . . .

PER SERVING:
Calories: 115
Fat: 6g
Protein: 9g
Carbohydrates: 6g
Fiber: <1g

. . . .

2½ cups chicken or vegetable broth, divided

1 tablespoon cornstarch

2 large eggs

½ teaspoon ground ginger

¼ teaspoon ground garlic

1 scallion, both white and green parts, thinly sliced

Ground black pepper

Low-sodium soy sauce

1 **Make the slurry.** In a small bowl, stir together ½ cup of the chicken broth and the cornstarch until smooth. Set aside.

2 **Beat the eggs.** In a small bowl, beat the eggs with a fork. Set aside.

3 **Cook the soup.** Pour the remaining 2 cups of broth into a medium saucepan, along with the ginger and garlic. Bring to a boil over medium-high heat on the stovetop or hot plate.

4 **Thicken and add the eggs**. Reduce the heat to low, so the soup simmers. Stir with a spoon to create a whirl in the middle and slowly pour in the beaten eggs. They should cook immediately.

5 **Finish the soup.** Gently stir in the cornstarch mixture and stir until the soup thickens, about 2 minutes.

6 **Serve.** Add the scallion and a drizzle of soy sauce.

TORTILLA SOUP

All the flavors of your favorite Southwestern dishes—tomato, corn, hot peppers, cheese, and corn tortillas—come together in this classic soup. This version uses shredded cooked chicken, but you can also try soy crumbles or cooked ground beef. Top the soup with sour cream or chopped fresh avocado for some extra creaminess.

4 cups low-sodium chicken broth
1 cup diced tomatoes (either canned or fresh)
¾ cup shredded cooked chicken or canned chicken
½ cup canned corn
¼ red onion, chopped
½ jalapeño pepper, sliced (optional)
1 lime, juiced
½ cup shredded cheddar cheese
8 to 10 tortilla chips, broken into small pieces

1 **Heat the soup.** In a medium saucepan, stir together the chicken broth, diced tomatoes, chicken, corn, onion, and jalapeño (if using), and bring to a boil over medium-high heat on the stovetop or hot plate. Reduce the heat to low and simmer to mellow the flavors, about 12 minutes. Remove from the heat.

2 **Serve.** Stir in the lime juice and serve topped with cheese and tortilla chips.

GLUTEN-FREE

Serves 2

PREP TIME:
8 minutes

COOK TIME:
12 minutes

STOVETOP OR HOT PLATE
MEDIUM SAUCEPAN
MEASURING CUPS
KNIFE
CUTTING BOARD
CAN OPENER

PER SERVING:
Calories: 374
Fat: 15g
Protein: 32g
Carbohydrates: 32g
Fiber: 5g

Love Your Leftovers:
The extra canned diced tomato, corn, and tortilla chips can be used to top a Buddha bowl or plain salad.

CHICKEN-VEGETABLE STEW

Spending hours waiting for a stew to cook can't happen with your busy schedule. Instead, try this recipe, which is ready in 20 minutes and still tastes homemade.

ı DORM-FRIENDLY
ı GLUTEN-FREE

Serves 2

PREP TIME:
10 minutes

COOK TIME:
10 minutes

MEASURING CUPS
MEASURING SPOONS
KNIFE
CUTTING BOARD

PER SERVING:
Calories: 359
Fat: 5g
Protein: 39g
Carbohydrates: 41g
Fiber: 5g

2½ cups low-sodium chicken broth, divided
1 tablespoon cornstarch
1 medium russet potato, peeled and cut into ½-inch chunks
¼ small onion, chopped
1 teaspoon minced garlic
½ teaspoon dried thyme (optional)
1½ cups cooked chicken, cut into ½-inch chunks
1½ cups frozen peas and carrots
¼ cup milk
Sea salt
Ground black pepper

1 **Make the slurry.** In a small bowl, stir ½ cup of the broth with the cornstarch until smooth.

2 **Combine the ingredients.** In a large saucepan, stir together the remaining 2 cups of chicken broth, the potato, onion, garlic, and thyme (if using), and bring to a boil over medium-high heat on the stovetop or hot plate. Add the chicken and frozen peas and carrots, and simmer for 10 minutes until the potato is tender.

3 **Serve.** Remove from the heat, stir in the milk and cornstarch mixture, and season with salt and pepper. Serve.

INSTANT VEGGIE NOODLE SOUP

Can you think of anything easier than just-add-water soups you can make in a flash? Make these your go-to lunch or study break treat for something quick and satisfying. Look for low-sodium bouillon powder or one that mimics stock because it tastes richer. Vegetable or beef stock works equally well. Get creative, swapping ingredients for more variety. For the noodle version, break up a ramen noodle cube into quarters and add a quarter to each jar.

1 tablespoon low-sodium chicken or vegetable bouillon powder
1 medium carrot, shredded
1 red bell pepper, chopped
1 zucchini, spiralized or cut into long noodles with a vegetable peeler
1 scallion, white and green parts, thinly sliced
Sea salt
Ground black pepper

1 **Make the soup jars.** Place the jars on your work surface and evenly divide the bouillon powder, carrot, red pepper, zucchini, and scallion between the jars; seal them, and place them in the refrigerator.

2 **Serve.** When ready to eat, boil water in an electric kettle, pour about 1½ cups into a jar, and let it stand for 3 to 5 minutes to soften the veggies. Season with salt and pepper and serve.

DORM-FRIENDLY
GLUTEN-FREE

Serves 2

PREP TIME:
10 minutes

COOK TIME:
5 minutes

VEGETABLE PEELER
BOX GRATER
ELECTRIC KETTLE
2 MASON JARS
MEASURING SPOONS
KNIFE
CUTTING BOARD

PER SERVING:
Calories: 64
Fat: 1g
Protein: 3g
Carbohydrates: 13g
Fiber: 3g

Smart Shopping:
Bouillon is a simple way to add flavor to soups, veggies, pasta, and sauces. Pick a low-sodium version and use it in moderation.

SAUSAGE-BEAN SOUP

Smoky sausage, tender beans, and a flavorful tomato-infused broth—what could be more enticing than that combination? Using cooked kielbasa means you don't have to cook the sausage, and it adds a rich, meaty taste to this soup. For an extra hit of iron and protein, add a handful of shredded kale before serving.

| GLUTEN-FREE

Serves 2

PREP TIME:
7 minutes

COOK TIME:
13 minutes

STOVETOP OR HOT
PLATE
MEDIUM SAUCEPAN
MEASURING CUPS
MEASURING SPOONS
KNIFE
CUTTING BOARD
CAN OPENER

PER SERVING:
Calories: 698
Fat: 36g
Protein: 33g
Carbohydrates: 60g
Fiber: 21g

**Love Your
Leftovers:**
This stew freezes
beautifully, so put a
couple servings into
sealable containers
and freeze for up to
2 months.

1 teaspoon olive oil
1 green bell pepper, cut into ½-inch chunks
¼ sweet onion, chopped
1 teaspoon minced garlic
2 cups chicken or vegetable broth
1 (14½-ounce) can diced tomatoes
1 (14½-ounce) can white beans, drained and rinsed
8 ounces kielbasa, cut into ¼-inch slices
Sea salt
Ground black pepper

1 **Sauté the vegetables.** Heat the oil in a medium saucepan over medium-high heat on a stovetop or hot plate. Sauté the bell pepper, onion, and garlic until softened, about 3 minutes.

2 **Cook the soup.** Add the chicken broth, tomatoes, beans, and sausage and bring to a boil. Reduce the heat to medium-low and simmer to mellow the flavors, about 10 minutes.

3 **Serve.** Remove the stew from the heat and season to taste with salt and pepper. Serve.

BISTRO TOMATO SOUP

Tomato soup does not have to be the pale, watery canned version; it can be a rich, comforting dish that will remind you of simpler times. Canned tomatoes allow you to get this on the table in 20 minutes and are almost as good as fresh. For a real childhood-inspired meal, pair this with a Stacked Grilled Cheese Sandwich (page 49) for dipping.

1 teaspoon olive oil
½ small sweet onion, diced
2 celery stalks, chopped
1 teaspoon minced garlic
2 cups low-sodium vegetable broth
1 (28-ounce) can diced tomatoes, undrained
1 (6-ounce) can tomato paste
2 tablespoons Italian seasoning
Sea salt
Ground black pepper

1 **Make the soup.** Heat the oil in a medium saucepan over medium-high heat on a stovetop or hot plate. Sauté the onion, celery, and garlic for 2 minutes. Add the broth, tomatoes, tomato paste, and Italian seasoning and bring to a boil. Reduce the heat to medium-low and simmer the soup for 10 minutes.

2 **Puree the soup.** Remove the soup from the heat and puree in a blender until the desired consistency. It is best just a little chunky. Add a little more broth if the soup is too thick.

3 **Serve.** Season with salt and pepper and serve.

GLUTEN-FREE

Serves 2

PREP TIME:
8 minutes

COOK TIME:
12 minutes

STOVETOP OR HOT PLATE
MEDIUM SAUCEPAN
MEASURING CUPS
MEASURING SPOONS
KNIFE
CUTTING BOARD
CAN OPENER

PER SERVING:
Calories: 229
Fat: 3g
Protein: 9g
Carbohydrates: 44g
Fiber: 13g

SPICY SEAFOOD STEW

GLUTEN-FREE
. . . .
Serves 2
. . . .
PREP TIME:
7 minutes
. . . .
COOK TIME:
13 minutes
. . . .
STOVETOP OR HOT
    PLATE
MEDIUM SAUCEPAN
MEASURING CUPS
MEASURING SPOONS
KNIFE
CUTTING BOARD
CAN OPENER
. . . .
PER SERVING:
Calories: 312
Fat: 8g
Protein: 20g
Carbohydrates: 38g
Fiber: 5g
. . . .

Smart Shopping:
Precooked rice packs
are your friend. They
are shelf-safe for
months, and you can
take out as much as
you need, reseal the
bag, and store in the
refrigerator for up
to 1 week.

This stew is inspired by the spicy, thick, flavor-packed soups of Louisiana with its shrimp, veggies, Creole seasoning, tomatoes, and rice. If you are not a fan of shrimp or cannot find it on sale, try chunks of cooked chicken and sausage instead.

1 tablespoon canola oil
¼ sweet onion, chopped
1 green bell pepper, coarsely chopped
½ cup shredded carrot (optional)
2 teaspoons minced garlic
1 to 2 teaspoons Creole seasoning
1 (15-ounce) can diced tomatoes, undrained
1 cup chicken broth
1½ cups coarsely chopped, cooked, peeled, and deveined shrimp
1 cup precooked white rice
1 tablespoon Louisiana-style hot sauce (optional)

1 **Soften the veggies.** Heat the oil in a medium saucepan over medium-high heat on the stovetop or a hot plate. Sauté the onion, bell pepper, carrot (if using), garlic, and Creole seasoning until softened, about 3 minutes.

2 **Cook the soup.** Add the diced tomatoes and juice, broth, shrimp, rice, and hot sauce (if using) and bring to a boil. Reduce the heat to low and simmer until the ingredients are heated through, about 10 minutes.

3 **Serve.**

BEAN & VEGGIE CHILI

Chili is among the top three meals for my kids and their friends, no matter what kind. Beef, chicken, turkey, and vegetarian, like this one, all make the cut, and there are never leftovers. Their favorite way to eat chili is spooned over tortilla chips and topped with cheese.

1 teaspoon olive oil

2 red bell peppers, coarsely chopped

¼ sweet onion, finely chopped

1 teaspoon minced garlic

1 to 2 tablespoons chili powder

1 (15-ounce) can diced tomatoes, undrained

1 cup canned red kidney beans

1 cup canned navy beans

OPTIONAL TOPPINGS

Cheese

Sour cream

Jalapeño peppers

GLUTEN-FREE

Serves 2

PREP TIME:
7 minutes

COOK TIME:
13 minutes

STOVETOP OR HOT
PLATE
MEDIUM BOWL
MEASURING CUPS
MEASURING SPOONS
KNIFE
CUTTING BOARD
CAN OPENER

PER SERVING:
Calories: 360
Fat: 5g
Protein: 18g
Carbohydrates: 64g
Fiber: 22g

1 **Soften the veggies.** Heat the oil in a medium saucepan over medium-high heat on the stovetop or a hot plate. Sauté the bell peppers, onion, garlic, and chili powder until softened, about 3 minutes.

2 **Cook the chili.** Add the diced tomatoes with their juices, and beans and bring to a boil. Reduce the heat to low and simmer until the ingredients are heated through, about 10 minutes.

3 **Serve.**

SPEEDY SUMMER GAZPACHO

DORM-FRIENDLY
GLUTEN-FREE

. . . .

Serves 2

. . . .

PREP TIME:
15 minutes

. . . .

BLENDER
MEASURING CUPS
MEASURING SPOONS
KNIFE
CUTTING BOARD

. . . .

PER SERVING:
Calories: 169
Fat: 5g
Protein: 7g
Carbohydrates: 30g
Fiber: 10g

. . . .

Variation:
You can add fruit such as watermelon, peaches, berries, or other veggies like radishes and hot peppers.

Cold soup could be a new concept for you, but give it a try because it is refreshing, flavorful, and packs a serving or two of veggies. This version is savory and summery with tomatoes, peppers, cucumber, and a delicious hit of basil pesto. If you can't stomach a cold meal, let the soup come to room temperature, and top it with a sprinkle of grated Parmesan cheese.

5 large tomatoes, coarsely chopped
1 English cucumber, coarsely chopped
1 red bell pepper, coarsely chopped
1 scallion, both white and green parts, coarsely chopped
2 tablespoons basil pesto
½ cup low-sodium vegetable broth
1 lime, juiced
½ teaspoon minced garlic
Splash hot sauce (optional)
Sea salt
Ground black pepper

1. **Blend the soup.** Combine the tomatoes, cucumber, red pepper, scallion, pesto, broth, lime juice, garlic, and hot sauce (if using) in a blender and pulse until pureed but still with a little texture.

2. **Serve.** Season with salt and pepper and serve. Store the soup in a sealed container in the refrigerator until you want to serve it.

ZOODLES WITH AVOCADO PESTO, PAGE 87

CHAPTER FIVE

VEGETARIAN AND VEGAN

MASTERING THE BASICS: DIY BUDDHA BOWL

With their picturesque layers and customizable, colorful toppings, Buddha bowls are a staple social-media food. But this dish goes beyond being a trendy creation to providing you with a balanced meal that won't break the bank. Use this simple formula to make your own Buddha bowls (and don't forget to share online and in real life).

1. **Choose a complex carb.** Start with 1 to 1½ cups of a complex carb, such as cooked grains (quinoa, rice, bulgur, oats), legumes (lentils, black beans, chickpeas), or starchy veggies (sweet potatoes, pumpkin, potatoes, winter squash).

2. **Choose a protein.** Try pre-seasoned tofu, tempeh, veggie patties or soy crumbles, hummus, hemp seeds, or legumes, if you have not used any of these in the complex carb layer.

3. **Choose some veggies and fruit.** Time to get creative! Chop the produce into strips or bite-size pieces, either cooked or raw, for easy eating. Try leafy greens, roasted vegetables, whole berries, or even leftovers such as coleslaw.

4. **Choose a dressing.** This component includes whatever dressing you think will go with the other ingredients, such as tahini, balsamic vinegar, salsa, or hot sauce. If you don't like dressing, add an avocado for healthy fats.

5. **Choose toppings.** This is the last layer in the bowl, which will boost the flavor and visual impact. Add chopped nuts, herbs, seeds, red pepper flakes, or crumbled nori.

FOUR-CHEESE MAC & CHEESE

My 18-year-old used to insist that I make his store-bought mac and cheese because I apparently could microwave better than he could. I understand the appeal of the no-brainer, neon-orange pasta, but my homemade version is gooey, melty, and requires only a few more minutes to make. Try adding your own fixings, such as chopped chicken, broccoli, or even soy crumbles.

1 cup water
½ cup small elbow pasta
¼ cup milk, 2 percent
½ teaspoon cornstarch (optional)
½ cup store-bought shredded 4-cheese blend
Ground black pepper

1 **Cook the pasta.** In a large microwave-safe mug or medium bowl, stir together the water and pasta and microwave for 3½ to 5 minutes, until the noodles are al dente. Drain the excess water.

2 **Make the sauce.** In a small bowl, whisk together the milk and cornstarch (if using), and then stir in the cheese. Add the mixture to the noodles and stir to combine.

3 **Cook the mac & cheese.** Microwave for 1 to 1½ minutes and stir until smooth and the cheese is melted.

4 **Serve.** Season with pepper and serve.

DORM-FRIENDLY

Serves 1

PREP TIME:
2 minutes

COOK TIME:
7 minutes

MICROWAVE
MEASURING CUPS
MEASURING SPOONS
SMALL MIXING BOWL
WHISK
LARGE MUG OR
    BOWL

PER SERVING:
Calories: 477
Fat: 20g
Protein: 22g
Carbohydrates: 51g
Fiber: 2g

Love Your Leftovers: Use your leftover cheese to make Cheesy Quesadillas (page 83).

EGG FRIED RICE

DORM-FRIENDLY
GLUTEN-FREE

Serves 2

PREP TIME:
10 minutes

COOK TIME:
3 minutes

2 MASON JARS
MEASURING CUPS
MEASURING SPOONS
SMALL MIXING BOWL
KNIFE
CUTTING BOARD

PER SERVING:
Calories: 336
Fat: 8g
Protein: 13g
Carbohydrates: 51g
Fiber: 2g

When I visited my older son's apartment, I was amazed by the teetering stack of take-out containers filled with leftover fried rice in the refrigerator. He loves it, orders it, and never finishes it all. So I showed him this foolproof method, and now he makes it at least a few times a week.

FOR THE JARS
2 cups cooked white rice (precooked package)
¼ cup chopped red bell pepper
¼ cup frozen peas
½ cup coleslaw mix with carrots
1 scallion, white and green parts, chopped

FOR SERVING
2 large eggs
2 tablespoons low-sodium soy sauce
1 teaspoon sesame oil
¼ teaspoon garlic powder

1 **Make the jars.** Evenly divide the rice, red pepper, frozen peas, coleslaw mix, and scallion between 2 mason jars. Seal and refrigerate for up to 4 days.

2 **Cook the rice mixture.** Unscrew the tops of the jars and cover them with plastic wrap. Poke a couple holes in the wrap with the tip of a knife. Microwave each jar on high for 1 to 1½ minutes until the rice is hot.

3　**Add the seasonings.** Whisk together the egg, soy sauce, sesame oil, and garlic powder and divide the mixture between the jars. Stir to mix the egg into the rice, re-cover the jars with plastic wrap, and microwave each jar for 1 minute to 1 minute and 15 seconds until the egg is cooked.

4　**Serve.** Let the fried rice stand for 2 minutes, fluff with a fork, and enjoy.

CHEESY QUESADILLAS

No barbecue or grill is needed to create this cheesy, spicy microwave-ready dish. Don't worry if the tortillas puff up like balloons when you cook them; this is normal, and they will deflate quickly. If you do have an oven or a panini press, use it to cook the quesadillas to get those tasty, signature char marks.

Olive oil for cooking
2 (6- or 8-inch) tortillas
¼ cup store-bought salsa
2 tablespoons sliced, pickled jalapeño peppers
1 scallion, white parts only, sliced
½ cup shredded cheddar cheese
Salsa, for serving (optional)

1 **Cook the tortillas.** Brush each side of the tortillas with oil, place them one at a time in the microwave, and microwave for 1 minute. Take them out and pat any excess oil off with a paper towel.

2 **Put the quesadilla together.** Place one of the tortillas on a clean work surface and spread the salsa evenly over it. Scatter the peppers and scallion on the salsa, and top with the cheddar. Place the remaining tortilla on top.

3 **Cook the quesadilla.** Microwave the quesadilla for 30 seconds on high, flip it over, and microwave for another 30 seconds.

4 **Serve.** Let the quesadilla rest for 2 minutes, then cut it into quarters. Serve with salsa, if desired.

DORM-FRIENDLY

Serves 1

PREP TIME:
10 minutes

COOK TIME:
2 minutes

MICROWAVE
MEASURING CUPS
MEASURING SPOONS
KNIFE
CUTTING BOARD

PER SERVING:
Calories: 516
Fat: 22g
Protein: 22g
Carbohydrates: 59g
Fiber: 2g

Variation:
You can add sliced tomatoes, shredded chicken, ground beef, sour cream, avocado, or bell peppers for a different flavor each time.

SINGLE-SERVE CHEESY LASAGNA

Serves 2

PREP TIME:
10 minutes, plus
10 minutes soaking
time

COOK TIME:
1 minute 30 seconds

ELECTRIC KETTLE
MICROWAVE
MEASURING CUPS
MEASURING SPOONS
2 LARGE (16-OUNCE)
  MUGS
KNIFE
CUTTING BOARD

PER SERVING:
Calories: 470
Fat: 20g
Protein: 21g
Carbohydrates: 55g
Fiber: 6g

Lasagna might seem like a whole-day culinary odyssey, but fresh noodles, sauce, creamy ricotta, and shredded cheese can be layered in a mug in minutes. Make a few and store them in the fridge for later.

1 fresh lasagna sheet, cut into 8 equal pieces
¾ cup ricotta cheese
2 cups chopped fresh baby spinach
⅛ teaspoon garlic powder
2 cups store-bought marinara sauce
½ cup soy crumbles (optional)
½ cup shredded mozzarella

1   **Cook the noodles.** Place the lasagna sheet pieces in a small bowl and cover with about 1 inch of boiling water. Let rest for 10 minutes.

2   **Mix the filling.** In a small bowl, stir together the ricotta, spinach, and garlic. If using soy crumbles, mix them with the marinara in a separate small bowl.

3   **Layer the lasagna.** Place mugs on your work surface and spoon ¼ cup of sauce into each mug. Top with 1 piece of pasta, then ¼ cup of the ricotta mixture, pressing down. Repeat 3 more times until all the ingredients are used up. Top the lasagnas with the mozzarella.

4   **Cook the lasagna.** Microwave each mug on high for 1½ minutes.

5   **Serve.** Let the lasagna sit for 3 minutes before enjoying.

CHEESY RISOTTO

Risotto is a dish that professional chefs take years to master, and while this isn't a perfect rendition, it is close enough to be impressive. The method takes a bit of supervision, but the cheesy, tender result is worth it. You can add 2 tablespoons of mushrooms, cooked sweet potato, shredded cooked chicken, or roasted red pepper to the rice and broth to pump up this basic recipe.

½ tablespoon butter
1 scallion, white part only, chopped
¼ teaspoon minced garlic
¼ cup arborio rice
½ cup vegetable or chicken broth
2 tablespoons grated Parmesan cheese
Ground black pepper

1 **Cook the veggies.** Combine the butter, scallion, and garlic in a large mug or microwave-safe bowl and microwave for 1 minute, stirring halfway through.

2 **Cook the rice.** Add the rice and broth and loosely cover with plastic wrap. Microwave on 60 percent power for 30-second intervals, stirring every interval, until the rice is tender and most of the liquid is absorbed, about 6½ minutes in total.

3 **Add the cheese.** Stir in the cheese and season with pepper.

4 **Serve.**

DORM-FRIENDLY
GLUTEN-FREE

Serves 1

PREP TIME:
4 minutes

COOK TIME:
6 minutes
30 seconds

MICROWAVE
LARGE (16-OUNCE) MUG OR MICROWAVE-SAFE BOWL
MEASURING CUPS
MEASURING SPOONS
KNIFE
CUTTING BOARD

PER SERVING:
Calories: 277
Fat: 10g
Protein: 9g
Carbohydrates: 40g
Fiber: 1g

Smart Shopping: Buy small quantities of rice to avoid having a big bag left over.

BURRITO BOWLS

Serves 1

PREP TIME:
15 minutes

LARGE MIXING BOWL
MEASURING CUPS
MEASURING SPOONS
KNIFE
CUTTING BOARD
CAN OPENER

PER SERVING:
Calories: 859
Fat: 31g
Protein: 31g
Carbohydrates: 119g
Fiber: 26g

Make It Yourself:
Homemade salsa is as simple as chopping 2 tomatoes, ½ red bell pepper, ¼ red onion, ¼ jalapeño pepper, and seasoning with salt and pepper. The salsa will keep in the refrigerator in a sealed container for up to 5 days.

Burrito bowls are the Southwest-inspired version of a Buddha bowl, so the layered ingredients might seem familiar. Combining complex carbs and protein will help keep you alert and energized for studying or running to classes. Put the bowl together the night before without the dressing and take it on the go, toss with the dressing, and enjoy.

1 cup cooked brown or white rice
2 cups chopped romaine lettuce
1 cup canned black beans
½ cup canned corn
¼ cup store-bought salsa
¼ cup shredded cheddar cheese
2 tablespoons sour cream
2 tablespoons store-bought dressing

OPTIONAL TOPPINGS
Chopped scallion
Jalapeño peppers
Hot sauce
Chopped bell peppers
Sliced avocado
Chopped cilantro
Chopped tomato

1   **Build the bowl.** In a large bowl, layer the rice, lettuce, beans, and corn on the bottom. Then arrange salsa, cheese, sour cream, and dressing on top. Add any other toppings you wish.

2   **Serve.**

ZOODLES WITH AVOCADO PESTO

Zoodles are spiralized zucchini, a light alternative to "real" pasta used in many gluten-free or low carb diets. You don't need a specific diet to savor this innovative twist on a classic favorite. Many grocery chains carry pre-spiralized zucchini, carrots, and squash in the produce section. You can substitute zoodles in any pasta dish, hot or cold, for a healthy, veggie-packed version.

¼ cup store-bought pesto

3 medium zucchinis, spiralized or sliced into ribbons with a peeler, or 4 cups store-bought spiralized zucchini

½ avocado, mashed

½ cup grated Parmesan cheese

Ground black pepper

Fresh basil, for garnishing (optional)

1 **Cook the "pasta."** Place a large skillet over medium heat on the stovetop or a hot plate. Add the pesto and stir to heat for about 1 minute. Add the zucchini and toss until the strands are tender and well coated, about 3 minutes.

2 **Finish the recipe.** Add the mashed avocado and Parmesan, and toss to combine.

3 **Serve.** Season with black pepper, garnish with fresh basil (if using), and serve.

GLUTEN-FREE

Serves 2

PREP TIME:
10 minutes

COOK TIME:
4 minutes

STOVETOP OR HOT PLATE
LARGE SKILLET
SPIRALIZER OR VEGETABLE PEELER
MEASURING CUPS
KNIFE
CUTTING BOARD

PER SERVING:
Calories: 338
Fat: 26g
Protein: 13g
Carbohydrates: 17g
Fiber: 6g

Dorm Hack:
Try it cold! Just toss all the ingredients together and serve.

COCONUT-CAULIFLOWER CURRY

GLUTEN-FREE

Serves 2

PREP TIME:
4 minutes

COOK TIME:
16 minutes

STOVETOP OR HOT
   PLATE
SKILLET
MEASURING CUPS
MEASURING SPOONS
KNIFE
CUTTING BOARD
CAN OPENER

PER SERVING:
Calories: 259
Fat: 13g
Protein: 9g
Carbohydrates: 32g
Fiber: 13g

My boys' friends request curry almost every time they stay for dinner because these types of dishes aren't common where we live. The delicious spice blend, tender cauliflower, and creamy tomato-coconut sauce tastes like a party in your mouth. Spoon this dish over rice or use microwave-warmed naan bread to wipe up every drop.

2 teaspoons olive oil
¼ sweet onion, chopped
1 teaspoon minced garlic
4 cups frozen, pre-blanched cauliflower, thawed
1 (15-ounce) can diced tomatoes, undrained
1 cup lite coconut milk
2 tablespoons curry powder

1   **Make the curry.** Heat the oil in a large skillet over medium-high heat and sauté the onion and garlic until softened, about 3 minutes. Add the cauliflower, diced tomatoes, coconut milk, and curry powder and bring to a boil. Reduce the heat to medium-low and simmer until the flavors mellow and the cauliflower is heated through, about 13 minutes.

2   **Serve.** Serve alone or over a microwaved package of precooked rice.

SKILLET MARINARA

Pasta is a weekly or even twice-weekly meal for my boys. They like all the different noodles and sauce combinations, but a humble herb-and-garlic-infused tomato sauce and long noodles make an appearance most often. This simple recipe can be made even simpler with a store-bought sauce, but homemade still tastes best.

2 cups vegetable broth
1 (15-ounce) can diced tomatoes, undrained
6 ounces spaghetti, broken in half
¼ sweet onion, chopped
1 tablespoon Italian seasoning
1 teaspoon minced garlic
Sea salt
Ground black pepper
½ cup grated Parmesan cheese

1 **Combine the ingredients.** Stir together the vegetable broth, diced tomatoes and juice, spaghetti, onion, Italian seasoning, and garlic in a large skillet over medium-high heat on the stovetop or hot plate.

2 **Cook the pasta.** Bring to a boil, reduce the heat to medium-low, cover, and simmer, stirring occasionally, until the pasta is tender, about 12 minutes.

3 **Serve.** Season with salt and pepper and serve topped with Parmesan.

Serves 2

PREP TIME:
3 minutes

COOK TIME:
12 minutes

STOVETOP OR HOT PLATE
LARGE SKILLET
MEASURING CUPS
MEASURING SPOONS
KNIFE
CUTTING BOARD
CAN OPENER

PER SERVING:
Calories: 502
Fat: 8g
Protein: 20g
Carbohydrates: 83g
Fiber: 7g

Variation:
Add chopped vegetables such as bell peppers or spinach to the skillet.

SPEEDY CHOW MEIN

DORM-FRIENDLY

Serves 1

PREP TIME:
5 minutes

COOK TIME:
8 minutes

MICROWAVE
ELECTRIC KETTLE
SMALL MIXING BOWL
LARGE (16-OUNCE)
  MUG OR
  MICROWAVE-
  SAFE BOWL
MEASURING CUPS
MEASURING SPOONS
KNIFE
CUTTING BOARD

PER SERVING:
Calories: 312
Fat: 3g
Protein: 13g
Carbohydrates: 61g
Fiber: 7g

Variation:
You can use rice noodles, fresh spaghetti, or ramen noodles instead of chow mein noodles. Just prepare them the same way.

Chow mein is a Chinese dish found in many restaurants and home kitchens around the world. In traditional recipes, the noodles are prepared separately and then added to the veggies and other ingredients. So even when making this dish in the microwave, you are still following some standard cooking practices!

2 ounces chow mein noodles, broken in half
½ cup coleslaw mix (cabbage and carrots)
½ cup bean sprouts
¼ cup frozen peas
1 tablespoon water
¼ cup store-bought chow mein sauce
1 scallion, white and green parts, chopped

1 **Cook the noodles.** Put the noodles in a small mixing bowl and cover with 3 inches of boiling water from an electric kettle. Let stand until the noodles are softened, about 6 minutes.

2 **Cook the veggies.** While the noodles are cooking, combine the coleslaw, bean sprouts, frozen peas, and water in a large mug or microwave-safe bowl. Cover with a plastic microwave cover and microwave until tender, about 2 minutes.

3 **Add the noodles.** Drain the noodles and remove the mug from the microwave. Add the cooked noodles, sauce, and scallion, and toss to combine and coat with the sauce.

4 **Serve.**

CLASSIC DAL

Dal might not sound very interesting, but it is delicious, or it wouldn't be a staple meal in India. This lentil porridge is created with inexpensive ingredients and is an excellent source of plant-based protein: perfect for getting you through a grueling study session or final exam without getting hungry.

1 teaspoon olive oil
¼ sweet onion, chopped
1 teaspoon minced garlic
1 (15-ounce) can lentils, drained and rinsed
1 (15-ounce) can crushed tomatoes
1 to 1½ tablespoons curry powder

1 **Cook the veggies.** Heat the oil in a medium saucepan over medium-high heat. Sauté the onion and garlic until softened, about 2 minutes.

2 **Cook the dal.** Stir in the lentils, tomatoes, and curry powder and bring to a boil. Reduce the heat to low, partially cover, and simmer until the sauce is mellowed and slightly thickened, 15 to 18 minutes.

3 **Serve.**

GLUTEN-FREE

Serves 2

PREP TIME:
5 minutes

COOK TIME:
15 to 18 minutes

STOVETOP OR HOT PLATE
MEDIUM SAUCEPAN
MEASURING SPOONS
KNIFE
CUTTING BOARD
CAN OPENER

PER SERVING:
Calories: 307
Fat: 4g
Protein: 20g
Carbohydrates: 54g
Fiber: 16g

Serving Tip:
Dal is often eaten plain but is truly delicious when combined with naan lightly warmed in the microwave for 10 seconds. You can scoop up every last bite.

SOUTHWEST-INSPIRED STUFFED SWEET POTATOES

Serves 2

PREP TIME:
5 minutes

COOK TIME:
10½ minutes

MICROWAVE
MEASURING CUPS
MEASURING SPOONS
KNIFE
CUTTING BOARD
CAN OPENER

PER SERVING:
Calories: 394
Fat: 8g
Protein: 15g
Carbohydrates: 69g
Fiber: 16g

Variation:
Try cooked ground beef, shredded cooked chicken, or chopped vegetables.

Many cultures have some version of a stuffed potato or sweet potato dish, and no wonder—they're an edible pocket for an assortment of almost any ingredients you like. This near-perfect comfort food was basically made for dorm-room cooking. All you need is a microwave and your favorite toppings to create a sweet, savory, or spicy (like this version) dish that can satisfy any food craving.

2 sweet potatoes, washed, dried, and pierced with a fork several times
1 cup canned black beans, rinsed and drained
½ cup store-bought salsa
¼ cup shredded cheddar cheese
2 tablespoons sour cream
½ scallion, green part only, chopped

1 **Cook the sweet potatoes**. Microwave the sweet potatoes for 8 to 9 minutes, turning halfway through, until fork tender.

2 **Stuff the sweet potatoes.** Cut the potatoes open, mash the insides with a fork, and then evenly divide the beans, salsa, and cheese between them.

3 **Melt the cheese.** Microwave the stuffed sweet potatoes again until the cheese is melted, about 1½ minutes.

4 **Serve.** Top with sour cream and scallion and serve.

PESTO SALMON WITH CHERRY TOMATOES, PAGE 97

CHAPTER SIX

SEAFOOD
AND MEAT

MASTERING THE BASICS: FRIED RICE

Fried rice is a staple menu item in most Chinese restaurants because it is inexpensive to make and variations are as easy as adding other ingredients to the base recipe. Here is the culinary blueprint for foolproof fried rice with egg:

1. **PREP YOUR AROMATICS:** Before you start cooking, mince 1 teaspoon each of ginger and garlic, and slice a scallion.

2. **PICK YOUR PROTEINS AND VEGGIES:** For proteins, try chopped chicken, shrimp, pork, beef, or tofu. For veggies, try frozen peas, carrots, or bell pepper. Chop everything into small pieces; you should have about ½ to ¾ cup of "add-ins."

3. **HEAT THE SKILLET OR WOK:** Heat a large skillet over medium-high heat; keep your heat high to prevent clumping. Add 1 teaspoon of your favorite vegetable oil (sesame complements the dish well; avoid olive oil because its flavor can be overpowering).

4. **COOK THE PROTEIN AND VEGGIES:** Add your protein, cook until done, then set aside. Add another teaspoon of oil to the hot skillet. Add the aromatics and vegetables and cook until crisp yet tender, about 2 minutes.

5. **ADD THE FLAVORINGS:** Add 1 tablespoon of soy sauce, ½ tablespoon rice vinegar, and 1 teaspoon sesame oil (if you aren't using this oil already). Cook for about 30 seconds.

6. **FRY THE RICE:** Add 2 cups of day-old, cool, cooked rice and the protein back in to the skillet and toss until heated through.

7. **COOK THE EGG:** Move the fried rice to the side of the skillet and pour 2 beaten eggs into the cleared space. Scramble the eggs, then gently fold them into the fried rice. Serve.

PESTO SALMON WITH CHERRY TOMATOES

Cooking fresh fish might seem intimidating, but it is moist perfection when blanketed in this flavorful pesto. The topping acts as an insulating layer between the flesh of the fish and the microwave, resulting in a garlicky, herbal flavor that accents the fatty salmon. You can also use a sun-dried tomato pesto if you prefer a slight sweetness to your sauce.

1 (5-ounce) boneless, skinless salmon fillet, rinsed and patted dry
Sea salt
Ground black pepper
1 tablespoon store-bought basil pesto or sun-dried tomato pesto
¼ cup halved cherry tomatoes
1 package microwave brown rice, for serving (optional)

1 **Top the salmon.** Season the salmon lightly with salt and pepper and place it in a small microwave-safe container. Spread the pesto evenly on of the fillet, then place the cherry tomatoes on top.

2 **Cook the fish.** Cover the container with plastic wrap and microwave for 3½ minutes. Check if the fish is cooked through; it should flake off in big chunks when pressed with a fork. If not done, microwave for 30-second intervals until cooked.

3 **Serve.** Serve the fish over the microwaved rice package (if using).

DORM-FRIENDLY
GLUTEN-FREE

Serves 1

PREP TIME:
5 minutes

COOK TIME:
3 minutes
30 seconds to
4 minutes
30 seconds

MICROWAVE
MEASURING SPOONS
SMALL MICROWAVE-
SAFE CONTAINER

PER SERVING:
Calories: 179
Fat: 5g
Protein: 30g
Carbohydrates: 5g
Fiber: 1g

CLASSIC TUNA CASSEROLE

Serves 2

PREP TIME:
5 minutes

COOK TIME:
10 minutes

STOVETOP OR HOT
PLATE
MICROWAVE
MEDIUM SAUCEPAN
MEASURING CUPS
MEASURING SPOONS
WHISK

PER SERVING:
Calories: 630
Fat: 37g
Protein: 30g
Carbohydrates: 44g
Fiber: 3g

Dorm Hack:
If you don't have a
microwave, the pasta
can be added with-
out reheating it. Just
add directly to the
sauce and increase
the cooking time by
about 2 minutes.

Tuna casserole is making a comeback in restaurants and on food blogs as a modest but delightful dish. Get dinner on your plate in less than 15 minutes with this version. The heavy cream creates a rich, thick sauce when combined with cheese, and coats the noodles and tuna for an easy decadence that will have you coming back for seconds.

1 tablespoon butter
1 teaspoon minced garlic
½ cup frozen peas
½ cup heavy (whipping) cream
⅓ cup shredded cheddar cheese
1 (8½-ounce) package fully cooked elbow pasta
1 (6-ounce) can solid chunk tuna (albacore or skipjack), drained

1 **Cook the vegetables.** Melt the butter in a medium saucepan over medium heat on the stovetop or hot plate. Sauté the garlic until softened, about 2 minutes. Add the peas and sauté until heated through, about 2 minutes.

2 **Make the sauce.** Stir in the cream and cheese and whisk until the sauce is thick and the cheese is melted, about 3 minutes.

3   **Heat the pasta.** While the sauce is cooking, microwave the pasta according to the package directions, about 1 minute on high to heat through.

4   **Finish the dish.** Gently stir in the pasta and tuna until everything is heated through, about 2 minutes. Try not to break up the tuna too much.

5   **Serve.**

PAN-SEARED TILAPIA WITH SALSA

GLUTEN-FREE

Serves 2

PREP TIME:
5 minutes

COOK TIME:
6 minutes

STOVETOP OR HOT
  PLATE
LARGE SKILLET
MEASURING CUPS
MEASURING SPOONS
SPATULA

PER SERVING:
Calories: 195
Fat: 7g
Protein: 31g
Carbohydrates: 4g
Fiber: 1g

Make It Yourself:
Store-bought salsa
is delicious, but
you can dress it
up by adding fresh
chopped tomatoes,
cucumber, mango, or
jalapeño peppers.

Fish is an excellent ingredient to include in your meal rotation at least once or twice a week because it is low fat and high protein, and an excellent source of vitamin D. This vitamin is essential for brain function and development. The pan-frying preparation in this recipe is a snap, and the salsa on top is fresh and satisfying.

2 (6-ounce) tilapia fillets
Sea salt
Ground black pepper
2 teaspoons olive oil
½ cup store-bought salsa
Lemon wedges, for garnish (optional)

1 **Cook the fish.** Pat the fish dry with paper towels and lightly season it with salt and pepper. Heat the oil in a medium skillet over medium-high heat. Add the fish to the skillet and pan-sear until cooked through and lightly golden, about 3 minutes per side.

2 **Serve.** Serve topped with the salsa and garnished with lemon (if using).

SHRIMP, VEGGIE & MANGO SPRING ROLLS

This recipe is a little technical but worth the effort. Shrimp sizing might seem confusing, especially when they are sold by "count." The count is just the number of shrimp found in one pound.

6 large peeled, deveined, cooked shrimp, coarsely chopped
1 cup shredded kale or romaine lettuce
1 red bell pepper, thinly sliced
1 mango, peeled and cut into thin strips
6 to 8 snow peas, cut into thin strips
1 scallion, white and green parts, sliced
4 spring roll wrappers
Water, for soaking
Store-bought Asian-inspired or tahini dressing, for dipping

1 **Arrange the fillings.** Arrange the fillings in separate piles on your work surface.

2 **Make the spring rolls.** Fill a bowl with warm water and place a clean kitchen towel next to it. Put 1 wrapper in the water for 15 seconds until pliable, then place it flat on the towel. Arrange ¼ of the shrimp and ¼ of the lettuce on the bottom third of the wrapper, leaving about 1 inch at the bottom. Place ¼ of the other fillings on the lettuce. Fold the bottom edge over the fillings, then fold the sides over the filling. Firmly roll the wrapper from the bottom up. Repeat with the remaining wrappers.

3 **Serve.** Slice the rolls in half and serve with the dressing.

DORM-FRIENDLY
GLUTEN-FREE
. . . .
Serves 2
. . . .
PREP TIME:
20 minutes
. . . .
MEDIUM BOWL
MEASURING CUPS
KNIFE
CUTTING BOARD
KITCHEN TOWEL
. . . .
PER SERVING:
Calories: 242
Fat: 1g
Protein: 13g
Carbohydrates: 49g
Fiber: 5g
. . . .

CRAB CAKES

Serves 2

PREP TIME:
10 minutes

COOK TIME:
6 minutes

STOVETOP OR HOT
  PLATE
LARGE SKILLET
MEDIUM BOWL
MEASURING CUPS
MEASURING SPOONS
KNIFE
CUTTING BOARD
CAN OPENER
SPATULA

PER SERVING:
Calories: 260
Fat: 11g
Protein: 23g
Carbohydrates: 17g
Fiber: 2g

**Love Your
Leftovers:**
Crab cakes are
scrumptious when
tucked into a pita
with shredded let-
tuce and a spoonful
of mayonnaise.

Tender, sweet crab cakes with pretty red pepper and scallion flecks and a hint of spice taste like they took hours to put together. In reality, these humble ingredients—canned shellfish, bread crumbs, and an egg—can be thrown together in very little time. Serve these cakes with a mixed green salad or rice for a heartier meal.

½ pound canned lump crab meat, drained
1 large egg
⅓ cup bread crumbs
1 scallion, green part only, diced
¼ red bell pepper, diced
1 teaspoon sriracha
1 teaspoon dried dill
Ground black pepper
1 tablespoon olive oil, divided
1 lemon, cut into wedges, for serving

1 **Make the crab cakes.** In a medium bowl, combine the crab, egg, bread crumbs, scallion, red bell pepper, sriracha, and dill until the mixture holds together when pressed. Form it into 4 crab cakes, each about ¾ inch thick.

2 **Cook the crab cakes.** Heat the oil in a large skillet over medium-high heat on a stovetop or hot plate and cook the patties until heated through and golden, about 3 minutes per side.

3 **Serve.** Serve with lemon wedges.

BUTTERED PECAN BREAD CRUMB COD

If you like fish and chips, this dish is a decent dorm-friendly stand-in with its buttery topping. The nuts add texture and a rich flavor and do not need the heat of the oven to create a golden finish. You can also try chopped cashews, almonds, or pistachios. Serve with precooked, seasoned quinoa prepared according to the package instructions.

3 tablespoons bread crumbs
3 tablespoons chopped pecans
1½ tablespoons butter, at room temperature
½ teaspoon dried thyme
2 (6-ounce) skinless cod fillets
Sea salt
Ground black pepper

1 **Make the topping.** In a small bowl, combine the bread crumbs, pecans, butter, and thyme until the mixture resembles coarse crumbs.

2 **Make the fish**. Lightly season the fish with salt and pepper and place the fillets in a 32-ounce microwave-safe casserole dish. Evenly divide the topping between the fillets and spread it over the top, pressing firmly.

3 **Cook the fish.** Microwave the cod for 4 minutes on high until the fish is cooked through. If the fish isn't done, microwave for 15-second intervals until cooked.

4 **Serve.**

DORM-FRIENDLY

Serves 2

PREP TIME:
10 minutes

COOK TIME:
4 minutes

MICROWAVE
SMALL BOWL
32-OUNCE
   MICROWAVE-SAFE
   CASSEROLE DISH
MEASURING SPOONS

PER SERVING:
Calories: 307
Fat: 17g
Protein: 28g
Carbohydrates: 9g
Fiber: 1g

Smart Shopping:
Many precooked grains can be microwaved in 2 or 3 minutes and are ideal accompaniments to many entrées. Stock up!

SALMON PATTIES

Serves 2

PREP TIME:
14 minutes

COOK TIME:
6 minutes

STOVETOP OR HOT
 PLATE
LARGE SKILLET
MEASURING SPOONS
MEDIUM BOWL
KNIFE
CUTTING BOARD
SPATULA

PER SERVING:
Calories: 373
Fat: 22g
Protein: 36g
Carbohydrates: 8g
Fiber: 1g

Salmon is firm enough, even canned, to create a satisfying meaty texture, so these patties could easily be used as burgers. Just make them a little bigger and pop one between a bun with a slather of mayo and a heap of shredded lettuce.

2 (5-ounce) cans boneless, skinless salmon, water-packed, drained
1 scallion, white part only, chopped
3 tablespoons bread crumbs
1½ tablespoons mayonnaise
1 teaspoon lemon juice
¼ teaspoon dried dill
Sea salt
Ground black pepper
1 tablespoon olive oil

1 **Make the patties.** In a medium bowl, combine the salmon, scallion, bread crumbs, mayonnaise, lemon juice, and dill together until the mixture is well combined and sticks together when pressed. If the mixture is too wet, add more bread crumbs, and if it's too dry, add a little lemon juice. Season with salt and pepper. Form the mixture into 4 patties, each about ¾ inch thick.

2 **Cook the patties.** Heat the oil in a large skillet over medium heat on the stovetop or a hot plate. Place the patties in the skillet and cook until crispy and browned on both sides, about 6 minutes in total.

3 **Serve.**

MIDDLE EASTERN-INSPIRED CHICKEN COUSCOUS

Middle Eastern food is famous for fragrant spices, tender meat, dried fruits, and wholesome grains. This recipe features lemony cumin- and cinnamon-infused couscous, studded with jewel-like red pepper. You might want to double the recipe because it tastes even better the next day and keeps well in the refrigerator for up to four days.

½ cup dry couscous
1 cup boiling water
½ teaspoon ground cumin
Pinch ground cinnamon
1 red bell pepper, chopped
1 scallion, white and green parts, sliced
¼ cup raisins
½ cup cooked or canned chicken, chopped
Sea salt
1 tablespoon chopped pecans

1 **Cook the couscous.** Put the couscous in a 32-ounce casserole dish and add the boiling water, cumin, and cinnamon. Stir, cover, and let stand for 10 minutes.

2 **Add the remaining ingredients.** Fluff the couscous with a fork and add the red pepper, scallion, raisins, and chicken.

3 **Serve.** Season with salt and serve topped with pecans.

DORM-FRIENDLY

Serves 1

PREP TIME:
10 minutes

COOK TIME:
2 minutes

ELECTRIC KETTLE
32-OUNCE
    CASSEROLE DISH
MEASURING CUPS
MEASURING SPOONS
KNIFE
CUTTING BOARD

PER SERVING:
Calories: 620
Fat: 8g
Protein: 33g
Carbohydrates:
106g
Fiber: 10g

Dorm Hack:
Boil the water in an electric kettle or coffeemaker.

CHICKEN ENCHILADAS

Enchiladas are a bit like burritos but cooked together under a layer of tasty sauce and cheese, which creates a creamy mouthful of tantalizing flavors. The enchilada sauce can be chili-based like the one in this recipe, or swap in a traditional mole or cheese sauce.

2 cups cooked or canned chicken, shredded or chopped
1 cup canned black beans
1 large tomato, chopped
1 (10-ounce) can store-bought enchilada sauce, divided
4 (7- to 8-inch) corn tortillas
½ cup shredded cheddar cheese

OPTIONAL ADD-INS
Canned corn
Chopped cilantro
Sour cream
Sliced jalapeños

1 **Make the filling.** In a small bowl, toss together the chicken, beans, tomato, and ⅓ of the enchilada sauce.

2 **Prepare the dish.** Spread ⅓ of the enchilada sauce on the bottom of a 32-ounce microwave-safe casserole dish.

3 **Fill the tortillas.** Place a tortilla on a clean work surface and spoon ¼ of the filling into the middle. Roll the tortilla up and place it in the casserole dish seam-side down. Repeat with the remaining tortillas and filling.

DORM-FRIENDLY

Serves 2

PREP TIME:
14 minutes

COOK TIME:
6 minutes

MICROWAVE
MEASURING CUPS
32-OUNCE
    MICROWAVE-SAFE
    CASSEROLE DISH
KNIFE
CUTTING BOARD
CAN OPENER

PER SERVING:
Calories: 592
Fat: 15g
Protein: 56g
Carbohydrates: 58g
Fiber: 14g

4 **Top the casserole**. Spread the remaining ⅓ cup enchilada sauce over the tortillas and sprinkle with the cheese.

5 **Cook the casserole**. Microwave the casserole until the cheese is melted and the enchiladas are heated through, about 6 minutes.

6 **Serve**.

CHICKEN STIR-FRY

Stir-frying is a speedy cooking technique that uses high heat and uniformly cut ingredients to create a balanced, tender-crisp meal. The use of precut veggies shortens prep time, but you can use whatever produce you have on hand or suits your taste.

1 tablespoon sesame oil

1 (12-ounce) package precut fresh stir-fry vegetables (broccoli, cauliflower, carrots, snow peas)

1 red bell pepper, thinly sliced

1 small zucchini, sliced

2 cups cooked or canned chicken

2 tablespoons low-sodium soy sauce

2 tablespoons honey

½ teaspoon ground ginger

2 cups precooked rice, for serving

1 **Stir-fry the veggies and chicken.** Heat the oil in a large skillet over medium-high heat on a stovetop or hot plate. Add the stir-fry vegetables, red pepper, and zucchini and sauté until they are crisp yet tender, about 7 minutes. Add the chicken and toss until heated through, about 2 minutes.

2 **Add the flavorings.** Add the soy sauce, honey, and ginger and toss to coat the vegetables, stirring for about 1 minute.

3 **Serve.** Cook the rice according to the package instructions and serve with the stir-fry.

Serves 2

PREP TIME:
10 minutes

COOK TIME:
10 minutes

STOVETOP OR HOT PLATE
LARGE SKILLET
MEASURING CUPS
MEASURING SPOONS
KNIFE
CUTTING BOARD

PER SERVING:
Calories: 640
Fat: 12g
Protein: 47g
Carbohydrates: 82g
Fiber: 6g

Smart Shopping:
Sesame oil tastes very strong, so a little goes a very long way. Choose a dark toasted oil, if possible; it has a fragrant, deep flavor.

SESAME TURKEY MEATBALLS WITH CUCUMBER SLAW

DORM-FRIENDLY

Serves 2

PREP TIME:
14 minutes

COOK TIME:
6 minutes

MICROWAVE
MEDIUM BOWL
SMALL BOWL
MEASURING SPOONS
KNIFE
CUTTING BOARD
BOX GRATER
16-OUNCE
  MICROWAVE-SAFE
  CASSEROLE DISH

PER SERVING:
Calories: 531
Fat: 21g
Protein: 43g
Carbohydrates: 43g
Fiber: 3g

These meatballs aren't your typical, Italian-herb-flavored kind; instead, you'll taste toothsome sesame in these little nuggets for something different yet familiar. The fresh cucumber slaw is like refreshing raita, a yogurt-based condiment popular in South Asian countries. Make sure you squeeze out as much juice as possible from the grated cucumber, or the sauce will be runny.

½ **pound lean ground turkey**
1 **large egg**
3 **tablespoons bread crumbs**
1 **tablespoon sesame seeds**
2 **(6-inch) pitas, halved**
½ **cucumber, shredded, with the liquid squeezed out**
2 **tablespoons plain Greek yogurt**
1 **teaspoon freshly squeezed lime juice**
Sea salt

1 **Make the meatballs.** In a large bowl, mix the turkey, egg, bread crumbs, and sesame seeds until well combined. Form the mixture into 8 meatballs.

2 **Cook the meatballs**. Put the meatballs in a 16-ounce microwave-safe casserole dish and microwave until cooked through, about 6 minutes, flipping halfway through.

3   **Make the cucumber slaw**. While the meatballs are cooking, toss together the cucumber, yogurt, and lime juice in a small bowl and season with salt.

4   **Serve.** Stuff the pita halves with 2 meatballs each and evenly divide the slaw among all 4 pita halves.

CHEESY CHICKEN PARMESAN WITH ZUCCHINI NOODLES

| DORM-FRIENDLY

Serves 2

PREP TIME:
10 minutes

COOK TIME:
4 minutes

MICROWAVE
MEASURING CUPS
MEASURING SPOONS
MICROWAVE-SAFE
   LARGE PLATE
MICROWAVE-SAFE
   MEDIUM BOWL

PER SERVING:
Calories: 808
Fat: 29g
Protein: 69g
Carbohydrates: 67g
Fiber: 8g

My boys ask me to double this recipe whenever it finds its way onto our weekly menu because these crunchy cutlets are very versatile. My older son stacks them on a crusty bun to create a bistro-style sandwich, and my younger one eats them cold right out of the refrigerator. They now make them at school and share them with their friends.

4 store-bought breaded chicken cutlets, fully cooked and thawed
1 (15-ounce) can or jar marinara sauce, divided
1 cup shredded mozzarella cheese
4 cups store-bought spiralized zucchini
2 tablespoons grated Parmesan cheese

1 **Cook the chicken Parmesan.** Arrange the chicken cutlets on a large microwave-safe plate that fits in your microwave. Microwave the cutlets on high for 3 minutes or until heated through. Spread ¼ cup of sauce on each cutlet and sprinkle each with ¼ cup mozzarella cheese. Microwave for 1 minute until the cheese melts.

2 **Cook the zucchini.** Put the zucchini in a medium microwave-safe bowl and stir in the remaining sauce. Microwave for 15-second intervals until the zucchini is tender and the sauce is hot, about 1 minute.

3 **Serve.** Serve the cutlets with the zucchini topped with Parmesan.

FIERY CHICKEN RICE NOODLES

Cold salads can be easier to make than an 8:00 a.m. class, even without a full kitchen. When I worked as a chef, rice noodles seemed so effortless because all they needed was a little soak in hot water to be tender. They also don't get soggy in dressings or sauces, so you can double the recipe and enjoy this salad on the second day.

2 ounces dry, thin rice noodles, broken in half

1 cup broccoli slaw or coleslaw mix

1 cup chopped cauliflower

½ cup shredded cooked chicken or 1 (5-ounce) can water-packed chicken, drained

1 scallion, white and green parts, chopped

¼ cup store-bought tahini dressing

2 tablespoons sliced almonds

1 **Cook the noodles.** Put the rice noodles in a small bowl and cover with boiling water from a kettle by about 3 inches. Let sit until the noodles soften, about 3 minutes. Drain, rinse in cold water, and transfer them to a medium bowl.

2 **Assemble the salad.** Add the slaw, cauliflower, chicken, scallion, dressing, and almonds to the noodles and toss to combine.

3 **Serve.**

DORM-FRIENDLY
GLUTEN-FREE

Serves 1

PREP TIME:
10 minutes

COOK TIME:
3 minutes

ELECTRIC KETTLE
MEDIUM MIXING
  BOWL
SMALL MIXING BOWL
MEASURING CUPS
MEASURING SPOONS
KNIFE
CUTTING BOARD

PER SERVING:
Calories: 664
Fat: 32g
Protein: 29g
Carbohydrates: 64g
Fiber: 7g

CHICKPEA CHICKEN TAGINE

GLUTEN-FREE

Serves 2

PREP TIME:
7 minutes

COOK TIME:
13 minutes

STOVETOP OR HOT
    PLATE
LARGE SKILLET
MEASURING CUPS
MEASURING SPOONS
KNIFE
CUTTING BOARD
CAN OPENER

PER SERVING:
Calories: 390
Fat: 9g
Protein: 31g
Carbohydrates: 51g
Fiber: 14g

Smart Shopping:
If you don't have garam masala on hand, you can substitute curry, cumin, or coriander.

A tagine refers to both the thick, fragrant, long-cooking stews and the cooking vessel in which they are made. Good news, though: You don't need a tagine to make tagine! This recipe is made in the microwave, but the generously spiced chicken, chickpeas, and tomato still taste as though they simmered for hours!

1 teaspoon olive oil
½ sweet onion, diced
1½ teaspoons minced garlic
1 (15-ounce) can low-sodium crushed tomatoes
1 (15-ounce) can sodium-free chickpeas, rinsed and drained
1 cup cooked chicken, cut into ½-inch chunks
1½ tablespoons garam marsala
1 cup shredded baby spinach or kale

1 **Cook the veggies.** Heat the oil in a large skillet over medium-high heat on a stovetop or hot plate. Sauté the onion and garlic until softened, about 3 minutes.

2 **Cook the tagine**. Stir in the crushed tomatoes, chickpeas, chicken, and garam marsala. Bring to a boil, reduce the heat to low, and simmer until the sauce thickens, about 10 minutes. Remove from the heat and stir in the spinach.

3 **Serve.** Try the tagine with naan for dipping, or spooned over pre-cooked rice or quinoa.

PAPRIKA CHICKEN

This recipe is a stripped-down version of chicken paprikash, a Hungarian dish of chicken in a paprika–sour cream sauce. The omission of the sauce means the meal is lighter and takes less time to make. Regular paprika is fine if you do not have smoked paprika in your pantry. If you want to cut the cooking time even further, you can cut the breast into two or three smaller pieces.

1 (6-ounce) boneless, skinless chicken breast
Sea salt
Ground black pepper
½ teaspoon smoked paprika
¼ teaspoon ground cumin
1 teaspoon olive oil
2 tablespoons sour cream, for serving

1 **Season the chicken.** Lightly season the chicken breast with salt and pepper and sprinkle it evenly with the paprika and cumin.

2 **Cook the chicken.** Heat the oil in a medium skillet on medium-high heat on the stovetop or hot plate. Panfry the chicken breast until cooked through and golden, about 8 minutes per side.

3 **Serve.** Let the chicken breast rest for 5 minutes and then slice it into 3 pieces. Serve with the sour cream.

GLUTEN-FREE

Serves 1

PREP TIME:
4 minutes

COOK TIME:
16 minutes

STOVETOP OR HOT PLATE
MEDIUM SKILLET
MEASURING SPOONS
SPATULA

PER SERVING:
Calories: 299
Fat: 15g
Protein: 39g
Carbohydrates: 2g
Fiber: 1g

Serving Tip:
Try this tasty chicken with the Mediterranean Couscous Salad (page 45) or Cauliflower Rice Salad (page 46).

KETCHUP-GLAZED MEAT LOAF

| DORM-FRIENDLY

Serves 2

PREP TIME:
5 minutes

COOK TIME:
12 minutes

**MICROWAVE
MEDIUM BOWL
SMALL BOWL
32-OUNCE
 MICROWAVE-SAFE
 CASSEROLE DISH
 OR SILICONE LOAF
 PAN
MEASURING CUPS
MEASURING SPOONS**

PER SERVING:
Calories: 623
Fat: 29g
Protein: 67g
Carbohydrates: 19g
Fiber: 1g

Meat loaf might remind you of home: hearty, simple, and packed with love. This recipe is equally delicious cold or warm, so try a thick meat-loaf sandwich when you need an afternoon pick-me-up. You can bake your meat loaf if you prefer; just pop it uncovered into the oven at 350°F with the glaze on and bake for about 25 minutes.

FOR THE MEAT LOAF

1 pound lean ground beef

⅓ cup seasoned bread crumbs

¼ cup finely diced sweet onion (optional)

1 large egg

2 tablespoons milk, 2 percent

2 tablespoons ketchup

¼ teaspoon powdered garlic

FOR THE GLAZE (OPTIONAL)

¼ cup ketchup

1 tablespoon vinegar

1 tablespoon brown sugar

TO MAKE THE MEAT LOAF

1 **Make the meat loaf.** In a medium bowl, combine the beef, bread crumbs, onion (if using), egg, milk, ketchup, and garlic until well mixed. Press the mixture into a 32-ounce microwave-safe casserole dish or silicone loaf pan.

2 **Cook the meat loaf.** Cover the dish and microwave until the meat loaf is no longer pink (160°F internal temperature), about 10 minutes. Take the meat loaf out and drain off any excess fat.

TO MAKE THE GLAZE

3 **Make the glaze.** While the meat loaf is cooking, in a small bowl, stir together the ketchup, vinegar, and brown sugar.

4 **Cook the glaze.** After draining the meat loaf, spread the glaze all over the top, cover the dish again, and microwave for 2 minutes.

5 **Serve.** Let the meat loaf cool for 10 minutes, slice, and serve.

SPAGHETTI SAUSAGE CASSEROLE

Serves 2

PREP TIME:
5 minutes

COOK TIME:
14 minutes

MICROWAVE
MEASURING CUPS
MEASURING SPOONS
32-OUNCE
    MICROWAVE-SAFE
    CASSEROLE DISH
KNIFE
CUTTING BOARD

PER SERVING:
Calories: 401
Fat: 17g
Protein: 18g
Carbohydrates: 47g
Fiber: 6g

Casseroles often use inexpensive ingredients, making them practical for a cook on a budget. This recipe is ideal to make ahead of time because you can store it, covered, in the refrigerator, and microwave it when you're ready to eat.

1½ cups store-bought marinara sauce
1 cup water
1 cooked Italian sausage link, sliced
5 white mushrooms, sliced
2 ounces dry spaghetti, broken into 2-inch pieces
1 tablespoon Italian seasoning
½ teaspoon garlic powder
Sea salt
Ground black pepper
3 tablespoons grated Parmesan cheese

1   **Mix the ingredients.** In a 32-ounce microwave-safe casserole dish, stir together the marinara, water, sausage, mushrooms, spaghetti, Italian seasoning, garlic powder, salt, and pepper until well combined.

2   **Cook the casserole.** Cover the casserole dish and microwave 10 to 14 minutes, stirring halfway through, until the spaghetti is tender, and the sauce is thick.

3   **Serve.** Let the casserole stand for 5 minutes with the lid on, then serve it topped with Parmesan.

PARMESAN PORK CHOPS

If you have ever heard of schnitzel—or tried it—you will now learn how to make it from scratch. Pork prepared in this manner stays moist and tender under its light breading and can be enjoyed plain or topped with a spoonful of applesauce.

2 (4-ounce) boneless pork chops, pounded to ¼ inch thick
Sea salt
Ground black pepper
¼ cup all-purpose flour
¼ cup grated Parmesan cheese
¼ cup bread crumbs
1 large egg
2 tablespoons olive oil

1　**Bread the pork.** Season the pork cutlets with salt and pepper. Pour the flour on a small plate and mix the Parmesan and bread crumbs on another small plate. Beat the egg in a small bowl. Dip the cutlets in the flour, coating them completely, then dip them in the egg, and finally in the Parmesan mixture until breaded. Repeat with the remaining cutlets.

2　**Cook the pork**. Heat the oil in a large skillet over medium-high heat on the stovetop or hot plate. Panfry the cutlets until cooked and golden, turning once; 6 to 7 minutes in total.

3　**Serve.** Put the cutlets on paper towels to soak up excess oil, then serve.

Serves 2

PREP TIME:
13 minutes

COOK TIME:
7 minutes

STOVETOP OR HOT PLATE
LARGE SKILLET
MEASURING CUPS
MEASURING SPOONS
SMALL BOWL
2 SMALL PLATES
SPATULA

PER SERVING:
Calories: 481
Fat: 27g
Protein: 33g
Carbohydrates: 24g
Fiber: 1g

Make It Yourself:
Place regular pork chops between 2 pieces of plastic wrap and pound with a can from your pantry to make cutlets.

CLASSIC SLOPPY JOES

Serves 2

PREP TIME:
10 minutes

COOK TIME:
9 minutes

MICROWAVE
MEASURING CUPS
MEASURING SPOONS
32-OUNCE
   MICROWAVE-SAFE
   CASSEROLE DISH
KNIFE
CUTTING BOARD

PER SERVING:
Calories: 453
Fat: 15g
Protein: 36g
Carbohydrates: 39g
Fiber: 3g

Love Your Leftovers:
The sloppy Joe mixture can be tossed with some cooked pasta or spooned over rice for a filling dinner.

I grew up with sloppy Joes as a regular menu item for dinner, then made them as a treat for my own kids at least once a month. Now they make these messy sandwiches frequently on their own. Don't get creative and add more tomato sauce, or the sandwich will fall apart entirely when you eat it. We learned that the hard way.

½ **pound lean ground beef**
¼ **cup chopped sweet onion**
1 **teaspoon minced garlic**
¾ **cup store-bought tomato sauce**
½ **teaspoon mustard**
Sea salt
Ground black pepper
2 **crusty buns**

1 **Cook the beef.** Combine the ground beef, onion, and garlic in a 32-ounce microwave-safe casserole dish, cover, and microwave until the beef is cooked through, stirring halfway through, about 6 minutes. Drain excess oil into a container and discard.

2 **Heat up the sauce.** Stir in the tomato sauce and mustard and season with salt and pepper. Cover and microwave until heated through, about 3 minutes.

3 **Serve.** Evenly divide the sloppy Joe mixture between the buns and enjoy.

KOREAN-INSPIRED BEEF LETTUCE WRAPS

Lettuce wraps are a popular street food in many Asian countries, featuring spicy fillings spooned into crisp fresh leaves. You can re-create this dish's distinctive flavor with some staple condiments like soy sauce, brown sugar, and sesame oil. If you use romaine leaves, cut out the thick rib running down the center so the leaf is supple enough to wrap around the filling.

½ pound ground beef
½ teaspoon minced garlic
2 tablespoons brown sugar
2 tablespoons reduced-sodium soy sauce
1 teaspoon sesame oil
1 teaspoon hot sauce
4 large lettuce leaves (butter or romaine)
1 scallion, white and green parts, thinly sliced

1 **Cook the beef.** Combine the ground beef and garlic in a 32-ounce microwave-safe casserole dish. Cover and microwave until the beef is fully cooked, stirring halfway through, about 6 minutes. Drain excess oil into a container and discard.

2 **Heat up the sauce.** Stir in the brown sugar, soy sauce, sesame oil, and hot sauce. Cover and microwave until heated through, about 2 minutes.

3 **Serve.** Evenly divide the beef mixture among the lettuce leaves and top with the scallion.

DORM-FRIENDLY
GLUTEN-FREE

Serves 2

PREP TIME:
6 minutes

COOK TIME:
8 minutes

MICROWAVE
MEASURING SPOONS
32-OUNCE
    MICROWAVE-SAFE
    CASSEROLE DISH
KNIFE
CUTTING BOARD

PER SERVING:
Calories: 314
Fat: 15g
Protein: 32g
Carbohydrates: 11g
Fiber: 1g

Variation:
For a spicy kick, add a pinch or two of hot pepper flakes along with the other sauce ingredients.

CLASSIC BEEF TACOS

ı DORM-FRIENDLY

Serves 1

PREP TIME:
10 minutes

COOK TIME:
3 minutes

MICROWAVE
SMALL MICROWAVE-
  SAFE BOWL
MEASURING CUPS
MEASURING SPOONS
KNIFE
CUTTING BOARD
CAN OPENER

PER SERVING:
Calories: 459
Fat: 19g
Protein: 37g
Carbohydrates: 36g
Fiber: 9g

Love Your Leftovers:
Toss leftover beans with cooked rice, chopped veggies, and Parmesan cheese to create an easy "kitchen-sink" casserole.

Tacos don't just have to be for Tuesdays or purchased from a fast-food restaurant; in a little over 10 minutes you can make your own whenever the craving hits. What could be better for an all-nighter energy slump? Tacos are just as satisfying with beans or ground chicken instead of beef. Try all your favorite fillings to create unique combinations.

¼ pound lean ground beef
1 to 2 teaspoons taco seasoning
2 small tortillas or hard taco shells
¼ cup canned black beans, drained and rinsed
¼ cup salsa
2 tablespoons chopped pickled jalapeño peppers
2 tablespoons sour cream (optional)
1 cup shredded lettuce

1 **Cook the beef.** Put the ground beef in a small microwave-safe bowl and microwave until fully cooked, about 3 minutes, stirring halfway through to break up the crumbles. Stir in the seasoning mix.

2 **Put the tacos together.** Place the tortillas on a clean work surface and evenly divide the seasoned beef, beans, salsa, jalapeño peppers, sour cream (if using), and shredded lettuce between them.

3 **Serve.**

PAN-FRIED SAUSAGE AND PEPPERS

This dish can be the base of many hearty dinners and lunches, as well as a meal of its own. The combination is a classic found in Italian cuisine but might be most well known in North America as the filling in a hoagie/sub/hero. Just throw on a slice of cheddar or American cheese, and you have the quintessential sandwich to keep you going well into a busy evening.

1 teaspoon olive oil
1 red bell pepper, thinly sliced
¼ sweet onion, thinly sliced
½ teaspoon minced garlic
2 (4-ounce) cooked sausage links, thinly sliced
1 teaspoon Italian seasoning
Sea salt
Ground black pepper

1 **Cook the veggies**. Heat the oil in a medium skillet over medium-high heat on a stovetop or hot plate. Sauté the peppers, onion, and garlic until softened and lightly browned, about 5 minutes.

2 **Cook the sausage.** Add the sausage and seasoning, and sauté the mixture until it is heated through and the veggies are lightly browned, about 5 minutes. Season with salt and pepper.

3 **Serve.**

| GLUTEN-FREE

Serves 1

PREP TIME:
10 minutes

COOK TIME:
10 minutes

STOVETOP OR HOT PLATE
MEDIUM SKILLET
MEASURING SPOONS
KNIFE
CUTTING BOARD

PER SERVING:
Calories: 693
Fat: 51g
Protein: 46g
Carbohydrates: 11g
Fiber: 3g

Serving Tip.
You can toss the sausage and peppers with cooked pasta and top with Parmesan for a more complete meal.

GUACAMOLE, PAGE 128

CHAPTER SEVEN

SNACKS *AND*
TREATS

125

MASTERING THE BASICS: TRAIL MIX

Trail mix is one of the handiest grab-and-go snacks for college students or anyone with a busy schedule. You can also use it as a topping for yogurt to add healthy fiber and protein. Store-bought trail mix can be incredibly high in fat and sugar, more like a dessert than a snack, and expensive. Homemade is more cost-effective, and you decide what goes in the mixture. Here is how to make a healthy trail mix:

1. PICK ONE CUP OF NUTS: If you have no allergies to nuts, pick out one or two types of nuts (whole or coarsely chopped) such as pecans, almonds, pistachios, walnuts, peanuts, or hazelnuts.

2. PICK ONE CUP OF DRIED FRUIT: Look for unsweetened, sun-dried fruit such as cranberries, raisins, cherries, blueberries, dates, mango, ginger, or apple.

3. PICK ONE CUP OF SEEDS: Look for raw or toasted unsalted sunflower seeds, pumpkin seeds, or flaxseed.

4. ADD FUN EXTRAS: This is where you can really customize your trail mix depending on whether you are making a sweet or savory mixture. Try ½ cup of dark chocolate chips, pretzels, wasabi peas, or popped popcorn.

PEPPERONI PIZZA DIP

Who knew you could eat pizza out of a bowl with chunks of soft bread? This dip basically lived in my refrigerator because I made it at least once a week for my boys. You can add your favorite pizza toppings, including chopped pepperoni, cooked ground beef or sausage, sliced mushrooms, olives, and even chopped pineapple. That last addition was my youngest's way of ensuring he had dibs on the entire bowl of dip.

4 ounces cream cheese, at room temperature
½ cup store-bought pizza sauce
½ tablespoon Italian seasoning
½ cup shredded mozzarella cheese
Bread chunks or tortilla chips, for serving

1 **Make the base.** In a small bowl, beat the cream cheese, pizza sauce, and Italian seasoning together until well blended. Spread the base in a 16-ounce microwave-safe casserole dish.

2 **Heat the dip.** Spread the mozzarella evenly over the cream cheese mixture and microwave until the cheese is melted and the dip is bubbly, about 2 minutes.

3 **Serve.** Scoop up the dip with bread or tortilla chips.

DORM-FRIENDLY

Serves 2

PREP TIME:
10 minutes

COOK TIME:
2 minutes

16-OUNCE
MICROWAVE-SAFE
CASSEROLE DISH
MEASURING CUPS
MEASURING SPOONS

PER SERVING:
Calories: 300
Fat: 25g
Protein: 10g
Carbohydrates: 11g
Fiber: 2g

GUACAMOLE

| DORM-FRIENDLY
| GLUTEN-FREE

. . . .

Serves 2

. . . .

PREP TIME:
10 minutes

. . . .

MEDIUM BOWL
MEASURING SPOONS

. . . .

PER SERVING:
Calories: 127
Fat: 11g
Protein: 2g
Carbohydrates: 10g
Fiber: 6g

. . . .

Smart Shopping:
If your avocados are
not ripe enough,
store them in a paper
bag with bananas,
which release a gas
called ethylene that
speeds up the ripen-
ing process.

Storage Tip:
Store any leftovers
in the refrigerator in
a sealed container
for up to 3 days. Stir
before using.

Knowing how to make decent guacamole is a culinary skill that will
serve you well with friends and family. This base recipe shows that
all you really need is a ripe avocado, a squeeze of lime, and a bit of
flavoring to bring this classic dish together. For a fancier version, add
chopped tomato, jalapeño pepper, chopped fresh cilantro, corn, or
roasted pumpkin seeds.

1 ripe avocado, peeled and pitted
1 lime, juiced
½ teaspoon minced garlic
½ teaspoon ground cumin
Sea salt
Ground black pepper
Tortilla chips, for serving

1   **Make the guacamole.** Put the avocado in a medium bowl and
    mash with a fork until it reaches the desired consistency. Add the
    lime juice, garlic, and cumin and stir to combine. Season with salt
    and pepper.

2   Serve with tortilla chips.

MICROWAVE POTATO CHIPS

My memory of the day I taught my kids to make potato chips in the microwave is crystal clear. They watched the microwave carousel with the attention usually reserved for their PlayStation. When a craving for crunchy, salty chips strikes you, this recipe will entrance you, too.

1 large russet potato, scrubbed clean
Nonstick cooking spray
Sea salt

1 **Slice the potato:** Fill a medium bowl with cold water. Use a knife to slice the potato as thinly as possible, placing each slice in the water. Soak the slices in the water for about 5 minutes, and then rinse in cold water until the water runs clear.

2 **Dry the potato.** Place a clean kitchen towel on your work surface and spread the slices on the towel. Place another towel on the slices and press until the slices are as dry as possible.

3 **Cook the chips.** Working in batches, arrange the slices in a single layer, not touching, on a microwave-safe plate lined with paper towels. Spray lightly with the cooking spray and sprinkle with salt. Microwave the chips on high for 3 minutes. Turn them over, spray again, sprinkle with salt, and microwave on 50 percent power at 30-second intervals until they are crispy and golden.

4 **Repeat in batches.** Repeat with the remaining slices.

5 **Serve.**

DORM-FRIENDLY
GLUTEN-FREE

Serves 1

PREP TIME:
10 minutes

COOK TIME:
10 minutes

MEDIUM BOWL
MICROWAVE-SAFE
   PLATE
KNIFE
CUTTING BOARD
KITCHEN TOWELS
PAPER TOWELS
SPATULA

PER SERVING:
Calories: 292
Fat: <1g
Protein: 8g
Carbohydrates: 67g
Fiber: 5g

ALMOST-CHEESEBURGER DIP

DORM-FRIENDLY

Serves 4

PREP TIME:
14 minutes

COOK TIME:
6 minutes

MICROWAVE
MEDIUM
MICROWAVE-
SAFE BOWL
MEASURING CUPS
MEASURING SPOONS
KNIFE
CUTTING BOARD

PER SERVING:
Calories: 309
Fat: 22g
Protein: 24g
Carbohydrates: 5g
Fiber: 1g

This dip makes more than one or two servings, but you will find it vanishes quickly when you take it out of the microwave. It also lasts in the refrigerator for at least four days. My boys scoop this out by the spoonful into tortillas and eat the wraps on the go before basketball games and work.

½ pound extra-lean ground beef
4 ounces cream cheese, at room temperature
1 cup shredded cheddar cheese, divided
1 scallion, white and green parts, chopped
1 teaspoon prepared mustard
1 tomato, chopped
1 large dill pickle, chopped
Tortilla chips or bread chunks, for serving

1 **Cook the beef.** Put the ground beef in a medium microwave-safe bowl and microwave until cooked through, about 3 minutes, stirring once to break up the crumbles. Drain and discard excess grease.

2 **Put the dip together.** Stir in the cream cheese, ½ cup of the cheddar, scallion, and mustard. Microwave until the dip is bubbly and the cheeses are melted, about 2 minutes. Top with the remaining cheddar and microwave for 1 minute more.

3 **Serve.** Top with chopped tomato and pickle and serve with tortilla chips.

PEANUT BUTTER CUP QUESADILLAS

You don't need to use fancy ingredients to create an energy-boosting snack. Bonus: this one tastes just like peanut butter cups! If you don't feel like microwaving or don't have this appliance, just make the quesadilla without heating the tortillas. The mini chocolate chips will be tiny pops of flavor instead of melted and gooey.

Nonstick cooking spray
2 (6-inch) flour tortillas
2 tablespoons peanut butter
2 tablespoons mini chocolate chips

1 **Cook the tortillas.** Spray each side of the tortillas with cooking spray, put them one at a time in the microwave, and microwave each for 1 minute. Take them out and pat excess oil off with a paper towel.

2 **Put the quesadilla together.** Place 1 tortilla on a clean work surface and spread the peanut butter evenly over it. Scatter the chocolate chips over the peanut butter, then place the remaining tortilla on top.

3 **Cook the quesadilla.** Microwave the quesadilla for 30 seconds on high, flip it over, and microwave for another 30 seconds.

4 **Serve.** Let the quesadilla rest for 2 minutes, then cut it into quarters and serve.

DORM-FRIENDLY

Serves 1

PREP TIME:
5 minutes

COOK TIME:
3 minutes

MICROWAVE
MEASURING SPOONS
KNIFE
CUTTING BOARD

PER SERVING:
Calories: 515
Fat: 28g
Protein: 15g
Carbohydrates: 53g
Fiber: 4g

Variation Tip:
You can dress this dish up with an assortment of ingredients such as bananas, a drizzle of honey, jam, dried fruit, or even candy such as M&Ms.

OLD-FASHIONED PEACH CRISP

DORM-FRIENDLY

Serves 1

PREP TIME:
10 minutes

COOK TIME:
2 minutes

MICROWAVE
SMALL BOWL
LARGE MUG OR
8-OUNCE RAMEKIN

PER SERVING:
Calories: 614
Fat: 24g
Protein: 6g
Carbohydrates:
101g
Fiber: 8g

Canned peaches might seem too pedestrian for a luscious dessert, but this inexpensive ingredient doesn't disappoint when topped with a cookie-like crust. You can also use fresh peaches, apples, or pretty much any fruit you'd like. However, if using fresh fruit, peel and chop the fruit until you have about 1½ cups total. When cooking, microwave for three minutes instead of two.

FOR THE TOPPING
3 tablespoons rolled oats

2 tablespoons brown sugar

1 tablespoon all-purpose flour

¼ teaspoon ground cinnamon

2 tablespoons salted butter, at room temperature

FOR THE PEACH BASE
1 (15-ounce) can peach halves or slices packed in juice, drained, and chopped

1 tablespoon granulated sugar

1½ teaspoons cornstarch

¼ teaspoon ground cinnamon (optional)

1   **Make the topping.** In a small bowl, combine the oats, brown sugar, flour, and cinnamon until well mixed. Add the butter and blend until the mixture resembles large crumbs. Set aside.

2 **Make the base.** In a large mug, combine the peaches, sugar, cornstarch, and cinnamon (if using) until well mixed.

3 **Top and cook.** Sprinkle the oat topping evenly over the base and microwave until the peaches are bubbly and the topping firm, about 2 minutes.

4 **Serve.** Let the crisp cool for 5 minutes and serve as-is or topped with ice cream or whipped cream.

CHOCOLATE CHIP AND PECAN COOKIE

Chocolate-chip cookies are a classic, never-fail-to-delight treat for countless college students, so a soft, sweet cookie, warm out of the microwave, is a no-brainer. If you have an issue with nuts, omit the chopped pecans. My oldest son, Mac, is obsessed with chocolate mint or peanut butter chips and often uses those instead of "plain" chips to create addictive variations.

DORM-FRIENDLY

Serves 1

PREP TIME:
5 minutes

COOK TIME:
45 seconds

MICROWAVE
LARGE MICROWAVE-
SAFE MUG
MEASURING SPOONS

PER SERVING:
Calories: 566
Fat: 29g
Protein: 12g
Carbohydrates: 68g
Fiber: 3g

1 large egg
2 tablespoons brown sugar
1 tablespoon butter, at room temperature
1 teaspoon granulated sugar
¼ teaspoon pure vanilla extract
5 tablespoons all-purpose flour
2 tablespoons semisweet chocolate chips
1 tablespoon chopped pecans
Pinch sea salt

Serving Tip:
This cookie is beyond decadent when served warm with a small scoop of vanilla ice cream, so go ahead and spoil yourself.

1 **Combine the wet ingredients.** In a large microwave-safe mug, stir together the egg, brown sugar, butter, granulated sugar, and vanilla until well mixed.

2 **Finish the batter.** Add the flour, chocolate chips, pecans, and salt and stir until combined.

3 **Cook the cookie.** Microwave the cookie until it is firm almost all the way to the center, about 45 seconds. Do not overcook.

4 **Serve.**

CREAMY ORANGE CHIA PUDDING

DORM-FRIENDLY
GLUTEN-FREE

Serves 1

PREP TIME:
10 minutes, plus
2 hours of soaking
time

2-CUP SEALABLE
CONTAINER
MEASURING CUPS
MEASURING SPOONS

PER SERVING:
Calories: 428
Fat: 17g
Protein: 16g
Carbohydrates: 53g
Fiber: 20g

Cooking Tip:
Try pressing a piece
of plastic wrap
directly on the pud-
ding surface while it
soaks to prevent a
skin from forming on
the top.

If you have never had chia pudding, the texture can be unfamiliar. It's like tapioca with a mild, slightly sweet flavor. The orange, vanilla, and creamy yogurt in this recipe create a luscious dish that imitates an orange creamsicle. Top this pudding with a mound of whipped cream for a fancy dessert.

¼ cup milk, 2 percent or nondairy
¼ cup orange juice (freshly squeezed preferred)
¼ cup vanilla Greek yogurt
1 tablespoon honey
1 teaspoon vanilla extract
1 teaspoon orange zest
¼ cup chia seeds

1   **Mix the pudding ingredients.** In a 2-cup sealable container, mix milk, orange juice, yogurt, honey, vanilla, and orange zest until blended. Add the chia seeds and stir to combine.

2   **Chill.** Seal the container and place it in the refrigerator for at least 2 hours or up to overnight.

3   **Serve.** Stir the pudding, adding a bit more milk if it is too thick for your preference. Serve.

PEANUT BUTTER AND FUDGE POPCORN

Popcorn is one of those ingredients that you can toss with almost any-thing, and the result will be delicious. This recipe is a sweet creation with a creamy peanut butter coating and streaks of melted chocolate. It is a messy snack, but well worth the extra napkins. Toss in some nuts, pretzels, and dried fruit to create different variations.

1 (3½-ounce) package plain microwave popcorn
½ cup mini marshmallows
¼ cup brown sugar
2 tablespoons butter, at room temperature
2 tablespoons peanut butter
2 tablespoons mini chocolate chips
Pinch sea salt

1 **Pop the popcorn.** Pop the popcorn according to the package instructions, for about 1½ minutes on high.

2 **Make the topping.** Combine the marshmallows, brown sugar, but-ter, and peanut butter in a medium microwave-safe bowl and cook on 70 percent heat for about 2 minutes, stirring every 30 seconds, until smooth and blended.

3 **Mix the popcorn.** Pour the popped popcorn into a large bowl and stir in the topping until well coated. Add the chocolate chips and salt and toss.

4 **Serve.**

DORM-FRIENDLY
GLUTEN-FREE

Serves 2

PREP TIME:
5 minutes

COOK TIME:
3 minutes 30 seconds

MICROWAVE
MEDIUM MICROWAVE-
    SAFE BOWL
MEASURING CUPS
MEASURING SPOONS
LARGE BOWL

PER SERVING:
Calories: 654
Fat: 42g
Protein: 9g
Carbohydrates: 67g
Fiber: 6g

Serving Tip:
You can also press the popcorn into balls while the mix-ture is still warm, to create cute gifts.

MAPLE CHEESECAKE PARFAITS

DORM-FRIENDLY
GLUTEN-FREE

. . . .

Serves 2

. . . .

PREP TIME:
10 minutes

. . . .

2 MEDIUM BOWLS
WHISK
MEASURING CUPS
MEASURING SPOONS

. . . .

PER SERVING:
Calories: 378
Fat: 31g
Protein: 7g
Carbohydrates: 20g
Fiber: 1g

. . . .

Smart Shopping:
You can use a pre-made whipped topping instead of whipping your own. Use ½ cup of the premade product and fold it in.

You do not have to use the oven when you want a delectable hit of cheesecake; this layered beauty is tart and sweet, and has a divine crunch from the chopped nuts. Honey works as a sweetener if maple syrup is out of your budget. You can also use crumbled graham crackers as a topping to stand in for the traditional cheesecake crust.

2 ounces cream cheese, at room temperature
¼ cup vanilla Greek yogurt
2 tablespoons maple syrup
½ teaspoon vanilla extract
Pinch salt
¼ cup heavy (whipping) cream
¼ cup chopped pecans

1   **Mix the base.** In a medium bowl, combine the cream cheese, yogurt, maple syrup, vanilla, and salt until smooth and blended. Set aside.

2   **Whip the cream.** In a pre-chilled medium bowl, whip the cream with a whisk until stiff peaks form, about 3 minutes.

3   **Make the mousse.** Add the whipped cream to the cream cheese mixture and fold it in carefully until the cream is incorporated and the mixture is fluffy.

4   **Serve.** Spoon the maple mousse into 2 small bowls or glasses and top with the chopped pecans.

BANANA SPLIT PUDDING

This dessert was the first thing I made as a teenager in the '70s, and it is still a terrific snack today. If you want to create different flavor profiles, try caramel or chocolate pudding instead of vanilla. You can also punch up the tropical theme by subbing in banana pudding mix and topping the parfaits with shredded coconut.

½ box vanilla instant pudding (102 grams)
1 cup cold milk
8 vanilla wafer cookies, crumbled
1 large banana, thinly sliced
1 cup premade whipped topping (Cool Whip, Reddi-wip)

1 **Make the pudding.** In a small bowl, mix the pudding mix with the milk. Refrigerate according to the package instructions until set.

2 **Layer the parfaits.** Put 2 glasses on your work surface and place 2 crumbled cookies at the bottom of each. Spoon ¼ of the prepared pudding over the cookies, followed by ¼ of the banana slices and ¼ of the whipped topping. Repeat the layers in each glass until all the ingredients are used up.

3 **Refrigerate and serve.** Place the parfaits in the refrigerator for 1 hour and serve.

DORM-FRIENDLY

Serves 2

PREP TIME:
15 minutes, plus chilling time

2 TALL GLASSES
MEASURING CUPS
KNIFE
CUTTING BOARD

PER SERVING:
Calories: 381
Fat: 12g
Protein: 6g
Carbohydrates: 65g
Fiber: 3g

Love Your Leftovers:
You can use the other half box of vanilla pudding to make yummy mug cakes. Simply add a tablespoon of the dried mix to the Chocolate Chip and Pecan Cookie (page 135) for a richer flavor.

NUT AND FRUIT SNACK BARS

DORM-FRIENDLY
GLUTEN-FREE
. . . .
Makes 8 bars
. . . .
PREP TIME:
15 minutes, plus
chilling time
. . . .
COOK TIME:
2 minutes
. . . .
MICROWAVE
8-INCH SQUARE
   BAKING DISH
LARGE BOWL
MEDIUM
   MICROWAVE-
   SAFE BOWL
MEASURING CUPS
MEASURING SPOONS
PARCHMENT PAPER
. . . .
PER 1 BAR SERVING:
Calories: 335
Fat: 13g
Protein: 6g
Carbohydrates: 52g
Fiber: 4g
. . . .

Granola bars are a popular choice for my sons when they need a quick energy boost and do not have time to spare. Store-bought bars can be packed with sugar and preservatives, so they prefer these homemade ones.

2 cups rolled oats
1½ cups crispy rice cereal
½ cup chopped pecans or almonds
½ cup dried cranberries or raisins
⅔ cup brown sugar
⅓ cup honey
¼ cup peanut butter
2 tablespoons butter, at room temperature

1 **Prepare the pan.** Line an 8-inch square baking dish with 2 pieces of parchment paper so that they overlap, and the edges hang over the sides of the pan. Set aside.

2 **Combine the dry ingredients.** In a large bowl, combine the oats, rice cereal, pecans, and cranberries until mixed.

3 **Combine the wet ingredients.** In a medium microwave-safe bowl, add the brown sugar, honey, peanut butter, and butter. Microwave for 30-second intervals, stirring between each interval, until the ingredients are well blended, about 1 minute. Microwave for 1 minute more and carefully remove the bowl.

4 **Mix the ingredients.** Add the wet ingredients to the dry ingredients and stir until well mixed.

5 **Make the bars.** Pour the oat mixture into the prepared pan and press it down evenly. Place in the refrigerator until firm, about 2 hours.

6 **Serve.** Pull the bars out of the baking dish using the overlapping parchment, cut into 8 (2-by-4-inch) bars, wrap them individually in plastic wrap, and store them in the refrigerator for up to 7 days.

MEASUREMENT CONVERSIONS

VOLUME EQUIVALENTS (LIQUID)

U.S. STANDARD	U.S. STANDARD (OUNCES)	METRIC (APPROXIMATE)
2 tablespoons	1 fl. oz.	30 mL
¼ cup	2 fl. oz.	60 mL
½ cup	4 fl. oz.	120 mL
1 cup	8 fl. oz.	240 mL
1½ cups	12 fl. oz.	355 mL
2 cups or 1 pint	16 fl. oz.	475 mL
4 cups or 1 quart	32 fl. oz.	1 L
1 gallon	128 fl. oz.	4 L

VOLUME EQUIVALENTS (DRY)

U.S. STANDARD	METRIC (APPROXIMATE)
⅛ teaspoon	0.5 mL
¼ teaspoon	1 mL
½ teaspoon	2 mL
¾ teaspoon	4 mL
1 teaspoon	5 mL
1 tablespoon	15 mL
¼ cup	59 mL
⅓ cup	79 mL
½ cup	118 mL
⅔ cup	156 mL
¾ cup	177 mL
1 cup	235 mL
2 cups or 1 pint	475 mL
3 cups	700 mL
4 cups or 1 quart	1 L

OVEN TEMPERATURES

FAHRENHEIT	CELSIUS (APPROXIMATE)
250°F	120°C
300°F	150°C
325°F	165°C
350°F	180°C
375°F	190°C
400°F	200°C
425°F	220°C
450°F	230°C

WEIGHT EQUIVALENTS

U.S. STANDARD	METRIC (APPROXIMATE)
½ ounce	15 g
1 ounce	30 g
2 ounces	60 g
4 ounces	115 g
8 ounces	225 g
12 ounces	340 g
16 ounces or 1 pound	455 g

COOKING LINGO

You might not know all the terms you see in the recipes, so here is a handy list of the most-used cooking terms:

BAKE: To cook in an oven with dry heat

BEAT: To stir quickly using a whisk, mixer, beaters, or spoon until the mixture is smooth

BLEND: To stir or mix two or more ingredients together

BOIL: To heat a liquid over a heat source until bubbling

CHOP: To cut into small pieces

DICE: To cut into small pieces; smaller than chopped

FRY: To cook in oil in a skillet or pan over high heat

GRATE: To rub ingredients such as cheese or veggies over the small holes in a grater to create fine shavings

GREASE: To coat a dish or pan with oil, butter, or shortening to prevent sticking

MELT: To heat a solid ingredient like butter or chocolate until it is a liquid

MINCE: To chop the ingredients into tiny pieces

REDUCE: To simmer ingredients down until there very little liquid is left

SAUTÉ: To cook food over medium-high heat with oil, broth, or water in a pan or skillet, moving and tossing frequently

SEAR: To brown the surface of foods very quickly using high heat

SHRED: To rub ingredients such as cheese or veggies over the small holes in a grater to create fine or coarse shavings

SIMMER: To bring liquids to a boil, and then reduce the heat so they bubble gently

SLICE: To cut ingredients vertically down, either thin or thick as specified by the recipe

STEAM: To cook ingredients in a perforated pan over simmering water or in an actual steamer

STIR-FRY: To quickly cook ingredients in a nonstick pan over high heat, using a little oil, water, or stock, and constant stirring

TOSS: To combine ingredients with a lifting motion

WHIP: To beat ingredients with a whisk or mixer to increase their volume and incorporate air

WHISK: To beat ingredients with a whisk or fork

ZEST: To remove the outer colored skin of citrus fruit using the small holes on a grater

INDEX

ACKNOWLEDGMENTS

Thank you to my family for inspiring me every day to work harder and learn more.

I am grateful to the Callisto Media team for their incredible hard work and for giving me the opportunity to work on many books with them over the years. They have helped me become a better writer.

Thank you to all the chefs, suppliers, farmers, and home cooks over the last 30 years who contributed to my knowledge of food and imparted their passion for exceptional ingredients and wonderful recipes.

ABOUT THE AUTHOR

Michelle Anderson is the author and ghostwriter of more than 50 cookbooks focused on healthy diets and delicious food. She worked as a professional chef for more than 25 years, honing her craft overseas in North Africa and all over Ontario, Canada, in fine-dining restaurants. She worked as a corporate executive chef for Rational Canada for four years, collaborating with her international counterparts and consulting in kitchens all over Southern Ontario and in the United States. Michelle ran her own catering company and personal chef business, and was a wedding cake designer as well. Her focus is food as medicine and using field-to-fork, wholesome-quality ingredients in vibrant, visually impactful dishes. Michelle lives in Temiskaming Shores, Ontario, Canada, with her husband, two sons, two Newfoundland dogs, and three cats.